Poems Are Hard to Read

Poets on Poetry   Donald Hall, General Editor

William Meredith

Poems Are
Hard to Read

Ann Arbor
The University of Michigan Press

PS
613
.M47
1991
157871
Feb. 1993

Copyright © by the University of Michigan 1991
All rights reserved
Published in the United States of America by
The University of Michigan Press
Manufactured in the United States of America

1994   1993   1992   1991   4   3   2   1

Distributed in the United Kingdom and Europe by
Manchester University Press, Oxford Road,
Manchester M13 9PL, UK

Library of Congress Cataloging-in-Publication Data

Meredith, William, 1919–
    Poems are hard to read / William Meredith.
        p.   cm.—(Poets on poetry)
    ISBN 0-472-09427-0 (cloth : alk.).—ISBN 0-472-06427-4
(paper : alk.)
    1. American poetry—20th century—History and criticism.
2. English poetry—History and criticism.   3. Poetry.   I. Title.
II. Series.
PS613.M47   1990
811'.509—dc20   90-45223
                                                      CIP

British Library Cataloguing in Publication Data

Meredith, William *1919–*
    Poems are hard to read.—(Poets on poetry).
    1. Poetry—Critical studies
    I. Title   II. Series
    809.1

    ISBN 0-472-09427-0

For Richard and Michael

Acknowledgments

The following poems are reprinted in "Reasons for Poetry" and "The Reason for Criticism" by kind permission of their original publishers or authors:

"This Is a Wonderful Poem," from *Collected Poems 1956–1976* by David Wagoner (Indiana University Press, 1978).

"Heroic Simile" copyright © 1974, 1975, 1976, 1977, 1978, 1979 by Robert Hass. From *Praise*, first published by the Ecco Press in 1979. Reprinted by permission.

"Five Men" copyright © 1968 by Zbigniew Herbert. Translation copyright © Czeslaw Milosz and Peter Dale Scott 1968. From *Selected Poems* by Zbigniew Herbert, translated by Czeslaw Milosz (Penguin Books, 1968), first published by The Ecco Press in 1986. Reprinted by permission of Penguin Books Ltd and The Ecco Press.

"Poem: On the Murder of Two Human Being Black Men . . ." by June Jordan.

"On Looking for Models" copyright © 1961, 1962, 1968, 1972, 1973, 1974, 1983 by Alan Dugan. From *New and Collected Poems, 1961–1983*, first published by The Ecco Press in 1983. Reprinted by permission.

"Traveling through the Dark" from *Stories That Could Be True* by William Stafford. Copyright © 1960 by William Stafford. Reprinted by permission of Harper & Row, Publishers, Inc.

"The Whipping," reprinted from *Robert Hayden, Collected Poems,* edited by Frederick Glaysher, with the permission of Liveright Publishing Corporation. Copyright © 1985 by Erma Hayden.

Contents

A Major Work

Poems are hard to read
Pictures are hard to see
Music is hard to hear
And people are hard to love

But whether from brute need
Or divine energy
At last mind eye and ear
And the great sloth heart will move.

—William Meredith

I

Memoirs

One of the High Ones: Some Recollections of W. H. Auden

The high ones die, die. They die. You look up and who is there?
—*Dream Song 36, John Berryman*

"So public a private man," my friend the poet Louis Coxe, with whom I first discovered his work when we were undergraduates at Princeton, has recently called him. Auden made a great deal of friendship and of privacy. For five years in uniform I admired the litotes of his remark on the eve of my being drafted: "I understand that one of the most trying things about the army is the lack of privacy." What greater sense of privacy could there be than is expressed in the poem "I Am Not a Camera"?

> Instructive it may be to peer through lenses:
> each time we do, though, we should apologize
> to the remote or the small for intruding
> upon their quiddities.

His position about the privacy of personal letters was set forth in a review of Oscar Wilde's letters ten years ago: "When we were young, most of us were taught that it is dishonorable to read other people's letters without their consent, and I do not think we should ever, even if we grow up to be literary scholars, forget this early lesson. The mere fact that a man is famous and dead does not entitle us to read, still less to publish, his private correspondence." And he instructed Edward Mendelson, whom he chose to be his literary executor, to place notices "in the American and British press requesting

Harvard Advocate 108, nos. 2–3 (1975).

any friends who have letters from me to burn them when they're done with them and on no account to show them to anybody else." I expect many friends will feel as Stephen Spender does, that they have no right to destroy letters that contain fragments and more of the thought and personality of an uncommon man. And I am convinced that this wish of Auden's had nothing to do with indiscretions in his letters. If he wrote indiscreet letters he was worldly enough to know that those are the ones that will turn up at Parke Bernet. Rather it was a surpisingly unworldly notion he had that destroying his letters would thwart the kind of personal biographer he despised, the kind who substitutes gossip for life of the mind.

As one of his executors, signatory to his published request, I burned my few postcards and letters, all except two that I'm not *done with* and working hard at rationalizing my right to keep: one speaks of designating me an executor and the other contains two poems, one of them still unpublished. I wake up at night and a friendly shade in the bedroom tells me both of these reasons are specious.

And what about the remarks from some of his letters that I copied in a journal before consigning them to *suttee* (the rite of the true hindu widow who cremates herself on her husband's funeral pile)? I hope the shade will forgive me these: they are words about or demonstrating his gift for friendship. "If I am loyal to my friends," he once wrote me, "it is because nobody I know has been as lucky as I have in the friends he has made. Only from one (he is famous and you can probably guess his name) have I been estranged, and that is a constant grief to me."

When Louis Coxe and I read him, back then in the late thirties, he became at once *our* poet, the poet of our generation. Coxe was writing a senior thesis on E. A. Robinson and I one on Frost. The sheer attractiveness of Auden as a poet rivalled those two older men's. (Frost and Auden remain the two poets of our century who mean most to me.) Coxe and I read him, at Princeton, ahead of most of our teachers chiefly because my sister, through an enlightened Marxist error that prevailed at Smith College, had discovered what I think it was

Spender identified as a mythical beast of the period, an *audenspenderdaylewismacneice,* and she sent me the first American editions of the four of them, including Day Lewis's manifesto, *A Hope for Poetry.*

In 1941 Muriel Rukeyser gave me a letter of introduction to Auden, and I went one afternoon, when I was a copyboy on the *New York Times,* to call on him in the house on Middagh Street where he lived then with Louis MacNeice and Gypsy Rose Lee, or so I believe and (what is more important, devoutly believed then): surely a more exotic mythical beast to beard in its den.

He was thirty-four. I felt half mythical for years after that nickel ride to Brooklyn. He was friendly and courteous. I said how much his poems meant to me and he said, "That's why one writes them." I told him I would soon be going into service and that's when he made the remark about privacy, which he pronounced with a short *i.* But I quote in its entirety the first intimate, now-burnt item of our correspondence, received soon after. It suggests a one-sided epiphany:

Dear Mr. Meredith
I'm afraid your poems are nowhere to be found in the house, so I fear they can't have arrived.

Yours sincerely,
Wystan Auden

The first real visit I had with him was in 1946. I was still in uniform when I ran into him and Chester Kallman at a performance of *The Magic Flute* (a work they would later make the best English translation of) at the Metropolitan Opera. We carped at the performance a little, as opera-lovers will. Not knowing we were in for twenty-one years of Rudolph Bing, we belabored some relatively lovable error of the then General Manager, Edward Johnson. It was a meeting of tastes, and I was invited to a Christmas party at Auden's second New York domicile at 7 Cornelia Street, in the Village. It was a heady experience. Edmund Wilson was there and I sat on the floor next to him. We drank from cheese glasses out of gallon jugs of red California wine—twenty-eight years ago that seemed remarkable to me—at that forerunner of the beautiful champagne parties he gave in the sixties at St. Marks Place. At one point Wystan confided in me that he was writing an autobiographical piece about his first love-affair. I edged away, thrilled. So public a private man. I edged closer. "Wait," he said, "let me show you some pictures." They were old sepia photographs of hydraulic machinery.

For the next twenty-odd years he gave those large, sociable parties, soon established on his birthday, February 21st. They were occasions people rose to, as if a magnanimity of the host raised or suspended our mutual expectation. I have been surprised more than once, meeting someone later whom I'd encountered casually there, to find that one or both of us had regressed severely in the harsher literary climate of New York. Wystan conferred excellence on us, much as he said saints do: "I have met in my life two persons . . . who convinced me they were persons of sanctity . . . in their presence I felt myself to be ten times as nice, ten times as intelligent, ten times as good-looking as I really am."

Just halfway through his life, as it turned out, he published a little essay in *Harpers Bazaar*—written for the money, I expect—called "Last Words." He tells of a patient of his father's "who kept tossing and muttering on his deathbed until he managed to gasp, 'Doctor, I want to apologize to you. Last time you came, I gave you a sweet biscuit with the sherry.'" He goes on:

> Whitman, Montessori (a permissive Italian educational theorist), the cocktail party, mass production . . . have ruined our sense of style by making us forget that being natural is every bit as much the fruit of disciplined cultivation as being mannered. For both are styles, and neither can be acquired unless it is consistently lived . . . The chief difference between the "natural" and the "artificial" style is that the former is so much more difficult to acquire.

He cites an instructive death. "Bert Savoy, the famous female impersonator, was watching a thunderstorm with some friends."—Isn't that a marvelous opening sentence for an anecdote? How would you complete it?—"Bert Savoy, the famous female impersonator, was watching a thunderstorm with some friends. 'There's Miss God at it again,' he exclaimed and was instantly struck dead by lightning."

He hedges about what his own last words would be, but admires Lady Stanhope's style:

> . . . I think often of ridiculous, crazy, incompetent old Lady Hester Stanhope whispering, "It's all been very interesting," and then dying far from home with her nose in the air. If when my time comes I can show even half as much courage, the mortician may paint me all the colors of the rainbow, the columnists come out every morning with an entirely new explanation of the World Crisis, and the telephone bleed to death under the stairs, but I shall not care.

That is, in fact, the style of some of his last words in verse, a poem published the week he died in the *New York Review of Books*.

No, Plato, No

I can't imagine anything
    that I would less like to be
than a disincarnate Spirit,
    unable to chew or sip
or make contact with surfaces
    or breathe the scents of summer
or comprehend speech and music
    or gaze at what lies beyond.
No, God has placed me exactly
    where I'd have chosen to be:
the sub-lunar world is such fun,
    where Man is male or female
and gives Proper Names to all things.

I can, however, conceive
    that the organs Nature gave Me,
    my ductless glands, for instance,
slaving twenty-four hours a day
    with no show of resentment

to gratify Me, their Master,
  and keep Me in decent shape,
(not that I give them their orders,
  I wouldn't know what to yell),
dream of another existence
  than that they have known so far:
yes, it well could be that my Flesh
  is praying for 'Him' to die,
so setting Her free to become
  irresponsible Matter.

What I had written him for his birthday in Berlin eight years ago, elicited by the remark in his letter about his good luck, was how I honored him for never having taken anyone off the list for those birthday parties. For him, loyalty was a simple, Blakeian corollary of the first acceptance of friendship. The *Bon Dieu* had given him better friends than anyone he knew, or what is perhaps more blessed and accurate, the *Bon Dieu* let him live and die in the belief that we were. In his presence and in his memory and in his work, we sense the expectation of such a friendship. It's something we can rise to.

Looking back on my friendship with him, I think music and especially opera was the subject I felt most at ease talking to him about. His learning and reading on other subjects was often intimidating, but not about music. On my last visit to Kirchstetten I remember saying to him that I felt instinctively that Strauss was a greater composer than Wagner because I take so much more delight from Strauss, and artists must be first judged as they give delight. The opinion didn't sadden him, as a disappointing ignorance might have. "Well, you're simply wrong about that, my dear," he said, and I was instructed for the rest of the evening, by precept and disc: one need not *prefer* Wagner, but one must acknowledge the larger and more original accomplishment. At the end, one reluctantly did.

When the late Noah Greenberg and his New York Pro Musica Antiqua were well-known but still causing new dazzlement to music-lovers, Auden was asked by the director to cast the speaking parts in Thomas Campion's *Somerset Masque*. Auden required of the poets he chose—Chester Kallman and I were among them—that they speak their lines from memory. My first public reading in my native city was the recitation of three seventeenth-century couplets:

> Thus with prodigious hate and cruelty,
> Our good Knights for their love afflicted be;
> But, o, protect us now, Majesticke Grace,
> For see, those curst Enchanters press in place
> That our past sorrows wrought: these, these alone
> Turne all the world into confusion.

Twenty years later, when the YM-YWHA celebrated its one hundredth year, I had the honor of memorializing Auden's life and work from the same platform.

In 1958, I invited Auden to a performance of Tchaikovsky's *Eugen Onegin.* I think this was the last time he went to the Metropolitan Opera, and he went reluctantly because of a growing list of grievances against Rudolph Bing, beginning with his production of *The Rake's Progress.* (It would be hard to imagine two men further apart in taste and style. Auden reported with approval the remark of Hofmannsthal's niece about Bing's production of Strauss's *Arabella,* in an English that made Hofmannsthal's elegant Viennese characters sound like the Bunker family, that *nothing was wrong with it except the style.*) (Who was the American industrialist who said, following the successful betrayal of his partners or employees, "Nothing has been lost save honor"?)

Anyhow, I wanted Auden to hear *Onegin.* To give Bing his due, it had never been performed at the Met before that 1957–58 season, and I thought it was a fine production. What I had not noticed was that between the many scenes requiring set changes, orchestral interludes had been composed to keep the audience in their seats. In the program it was reported that these had been "suggested by Mr. Mitropoulos," but I mistrust that because Dmitri Mitropoulos, who never conducted from a score, who once said that if he didn't know a work well enough to conduct it without a score he didn't know it well enough to have an opinion about it, pored continuously over the score as he conducted these "musical interludes."

They consisted in rather obvious repetitions of what might be called the hit tunes of the opera, and Tchaikovsky was not a composer to let go of a melody before he'd got his money's worth out of it. The first of these ersatz pieces was loud and vulgar in a fairly ravishing way, and I was sitting there next to Wystan in the gold cave, letting it pour over me like expensive after-shave lotion, unaware of the force of critical rage that was generating beside me. At the noisy end of the piece there was huge applause—nothing that *easy* had happened to this audience in a long time and they were grateful. As the applause faded, a high British voice which I was proud and horrified to realize was my guest's voice—we were in the box of the Metropolitan Opera Club—was heard through the house calling *Shame! Shame!*

It did no good to explain afterwards (*Who* is Meredith's guest? echoed in the high-ceilinged club room during the intermission) that he was one of the librettists of *The Rake's Progress.* Mostly we didn't like modern opera. To a man we were too cowardly to call out disapproval. And which of us would wear sneakers with his dinner-jacket?

He was eccentric in a way that reproved unthinking or timid conformity. He wrote, "Bad art is always with us, but any given work of art is always bad in a period way: the particular kind of badness it exhibits will pass away to be succeeded by some other kind. It is unnecessary, therefore, to attack it, because it will perish anyhow." But he couldn't sit silent—in fact he had to shatter the social decorum he attached a good deal of importance to—when a musical forgery was being applauded.

There are things I know about Auden, as there are a few I know about Robert Frost, that I will never write down and, if I should tell them again, will tell in confidence. This is not because of loyalty or an exaggerated sense of honor, but because those two men had a sense of privacy that maintains itself past the grave. If you got the message of their personalities, that was an essential part of the message.

Both men, in a way that isn't common among modern artists, had a personal sense of the past. Spender has written of Auden, "he was extremely interested in the stream of events

called 'History', and in analysing people and relationships."
Frost spoke of history as *gossip*. Both men relished gossip, past
and present, the way I suppose Shakespeare did.

And both men did and said occasional mean-spirited or
worse things, like you and me. Some of these could be
mocked, some could be condemned. It would be a kind of lie
to recount such words and deeds, since they run quite counter
to the deliberate life and work of each man. But that isn't why
I refrain from recounting them. I refrain from recounting
them because I'd like to associate myself with these two extra-
ordinary men, after their deaths, in a way that suggests I
understood them a little, as great men can be understood by
ordinary men, personally.

Auden's poems take us all into the kind of confidence that
is better than gossip. "That's why one writes them." In "The
Garrison" the reader must feel he is one of *the choir we sort
with,* otherwise why is the poem so intimate?

> We, Chester,
> and the choir we sort with have been assigned to
> garrison stations.
>
> Whoever rules, our duty to the City
> is loyal opposition, never greening
> for the big money, never neighing after
> a public image.
>
> Let us leave rebellions to the choleric
> who enjoy them: to serve as a paradigm
> now of what a plausible Future might be
> is what we're here for.

The personality that became so distinct and attractive in
the later poems is the one we are left to marvel at and gossip
about to our hearts' content.

In Loving Memory of the Late
Author of the Dream Songs

In their late eighties, Severn and Trelawny were laid to rest in the *Cimitero Acattolico* in Rome beside the young men whose genius had been the chief events of their lives, Keats dead at twenty-six, Shelley at twenty-nine. What a crowd of us there would be, by that criterion, in John Berryman's graveyard—men and women who survive him knowing that their encounters with him constitute an identity, whatever other identities we achieve before the grave.

A man does not want to jostle or seem proprietary in speaking of such friendship. Dozens of us appear by our right names in his poems, the only disclaimer is the mystifying one for Henry himself "(not the poet, not me)," but nobody sues. Probably the impulse to bear witness should take as its tone the agonized modesty of one of his last poems:

> Happy to be here
> and to have been here, with such lovely ones
> so infinitely better.

I knew him first after World War II when I was teaching and doing some rather casual graduate work at Princeton. The appointment as R. P. Blackmur's assistant in the creative writing courses at the university was an annual one, that is, one person couldn't hold it for more than one year consecutively, and for several years Berryman and I held it alternately.

Virginia Quarterly Review 49, no. 1 (1973).

But we were not friends then. He was formidable in his learning and in his pride of learning, I was even less read then than now. We had many friends in common, but we kept at the opposite ends of parties or perhaps only I did. If we liked anything about one another it was the jokes we made.

The friendship that came about suddenly and remains a chief event in my life started in Vermont in the summer of 1962 at the Bread Loaf School of English. We lived under the same roof there for six weeks, with most of the other faculty, in a big summer "cottage" in the mountains. The fact that he and I drank gin at noon, which had to be elaborately overlooked and was, when that was possible, may have thrown us together at first. But the lucid fact of Kate Berryman, during that summer as during the whole last decade of his life, translated what was difficult about John into terms that less extraordinary people could understand. From the start, my friendship was always with both Kate and John, and I will never know how much I owe it to her translations of him and me, especially at the start.

Berryman came to know Robert Frost that summer, visiting him (and the close friends of his later years, the Theodore Morrisons) at the Homer Noble Farm, a mile down the road from the Bread Loaf campus. There were not many visits, but he came close to Frost. (Besides the "Three around the Old Gentleman," there are two other references to these visits in *The Dream Songs* and one in "Delusions, Etc.") If I had to guess what Frost liked best about him, I would say either his edgy wit or his knowledge of American history or his wife. The meetings were notable because Frost did not generally take to younger poets with egos the size of his own, and accomplishments to support them, but he took to Berryman.

At the beginning of the summer John gave a reading at the school. He started off with a recitation from memory of Frost's "The Oven Bird," an early poem I had long felt was a key to Frost's diction, the colloquial language that once astonished readers; in two lines especially:

> The bird would cease and be as other birds
> But that he knows in singing not to sing.

This was before John's first visit to the cabin. In other words, he was not one of Bread Loaf's summer converts but a man who lived with Frost's work, as I did. I think this was one of our first expressed affinities.

That evening was the first time I had heard "Dream Songs" read, though I was to hear them at all hours for the next several weeks. Once he came to my room at 4 A.M. for what was supposed to be a private reading of a song just finished. The acoustics of the big wooden house made it an unpopular public event. When John read aloud, the etymology of the word *aloud* was brought forcibly home.

We spent many hours of those days and nights together. Kate was pregnant, but to be sociable she sometimes drank some of the gallon jug of Gallo or Italian Swiss Colony sherry with which extraordinarily (a habit from the wartime drouth?) our martinis were always made. The Berrymans had many friends, students and faculty. The "Dream Songs" were new to all of us then, and John would read the new ones that were birthing week by week as another man might tell anecdotes. The anecdotal quality of them emerged in his readings: it was the character of Henry who dangled from strings and told you his droll, outrageous life.

It was not until the end of that summer of '62 that Berryman made a serious attempt to find the structure of what I think had been, up to then, an improvisational work. He and Kate lingered a few weeks after the summer session, in a cabin further up the valley belonging to a remarkable lady who has befriended many writers, including this one, Mrs. Frank A. Scott. There John set in order for the first time the contents of a small brown suitcase that contained, in profuse disorder, a literary event of 1964. "Dream Song 62" records a brief philosophical exchange he had at this time with a rabbit, outside the cabin. He worked there until it was time for him to go to Providence in September, where that year he taught Edwin Honig's courses at Brown University.

I move now to the last visit I had with him. In May of 1971 he was invited, with a number of other poets, to a kind of poetry festival at Goddard College in northern Vermont.

I drove from New London to pick him up in Hartford, and we planned to go on to my house at Bread Loaf. But the aging Mercedes that I affect lost a carburetor on the way, and we stayed at Woodstock that night. His talk was rangy, but returned to religion ("the idiot temptation to try to live the Christian life" is a phrase I remember) and to the disease of alcoholism, from which he felt he had at last been cured. He who would never wear decorations was wearing a rosette: the badge of three months' abstinence, from Alcoholics Anonymous. Walking late in a cold mist, he stopped once on a sedate nineteenth-century street of that handsome town and spoke, in a voice that made windows go up in the quiet night, the legend he had decided on for his tombstone. It was to say simply: John Berryman, 1914–19—— ("There's no particular hurry about that last date,") and then, very loud: "Fantastic! Fantastic! Thank Thee, Dear Lord!" We shared a room that night at the Woodstock Inn. I had forgotten the terrible intensity of his cigarette cough.

After lunch the next day, two Goddard students came to drive us the last sixty or seventy-five miles to Plainfield. At one point in the drive, and I can't remember how he came to the remark, he said, "You and I are the last of the unreconstructed snobs, Meredith." Partly it was said to shock the pleasantly reconstructed students, a young man and a young woman. (She drove like a liberated woman. They were both bright.) But remembering the remark makes me aware now of another affinity between Berryman and myself, a yearning for decorum, even for old-fashioned manners. I'm not speaking about our social behavior, which is dubious in both cases, but about a social ideal. At heart, Berryman was a courtly man, though usually (like most of us) he could act out only a parody of that. The forms of behavior that attracted him were as traditional as the forms of prosody.

He took a long, deliberate time to master prosody. The terza rima of "Canto Amor" (1946) is virtuoso, self-conscious still. Some of the Petrarchan "Sonnets," which date from the same decade, are slightly contrived. Even in the "Dream

Songs" there are occasional lines that seem to have rhymed themselves wilfully into existence:

> At Harvard & Yale must Pussy-cat be heard
> in the dead of winter when we must be sad
> and feel by the weather had.

But what makes the prosody consistently astonishing, from beginning to end (see, in the last book, the form of "Scholar at the Orchid Pavilion" and "He Resigns"), is the sense of individual selection of the form for each poem. Even in the ones where you feel an excess of formality, like the "Canto Amor," or in a particular sonnet where the tradition seems to go sterile, or in a Dream Song where there is an effect of doggerel, the flaw is appropriate to the feeling of the poem and is not really a flaw but a felt, if not a calculated, effect.

Throughout his work there seems to have been an absolute and passive attention to the poem's identity, which produced this accuracy of form. It is an accuracy that dims noticeably in certain poems in the last two books—poems which could be described on the one hand as wilful or unmannerly, on the other hand as deeply troubled. They represent a wrestling with new beginnings, I think, an agony of genius renewing itself. One does not patronize them by saying that the last two books are greatly flawed, the adverb cuts both ways. The prosody is violent, the enterprise is desperate, but the work is not clumsy. The poet is paying his kind of absolute attention to *scrannel* sounds, to use the word from "Lycidas."

Social decorum as it existed at Cambridge when he went to England in 1936 must have seemed trustworthy to him (although his taste never failed him worse than when he wrote about those days in "Love & Fame"). Manners in the larger sense were for him an agreed-on language, an established position from which you could negotiate with accuracy toward or away from human intimacy. Without such fixes (taking the term from navigation) the maneuver is more perilous than with them. He must have picked up the reassuring starchiness of his British spelling and idiom at this time. To the end he would speak of having been *in hospital*, he spelt honor *honour,* he would have addressed an insulting letter "Jerry Rubin, Esq." Society and its language were for him still a tissue of contracts, however much in flux, however headlong in decline. Once when he wanted to swear at a good man who had with considerable justification asked our party to leave his restaurant, Berryman called him an insolent innkeeper, indicating outrage at the specific breach of contract he felt he had suffered.

I think that day in Vermont he had been speaking against the promiscuous honesty that is preferred to conventional manners today, an honesty that is often no more than an evasion of the social predicament. It pretends to candor but doesn't care enough about the particular human engagement to look you in the eye, doesn't seem to recognize that all honest engagements are negotiations, *ad hominem* negotiations that require the expense of attention. And it is this kind of attention that distinguishes Berryman's poems. They meet the eye, they pay you that courtesy.

And calculated rudeness, an element of the Berryman rhetoric, is possible only for the mannerly. It works in terms of contracts and just deserts:

> Many a one his pen's been bad unto,
> which they deserved.

Expressions of contempt in modern literature often smack of self-contempt, contempt for the human tribe. Berryman's contempt is for aberrations from the inherited good manners of the tribe. "I saw in my dream the great lost cities, Macchu Picchu, Cambridge Mass., Angkor...." It is a curious fact about modern poetry that many of its large figures have been men of enormous intelligence (we couldn't have made good use of Tennyson) supported by enormous reading, and that they want to restore rather than overthrow traditions. With our lesser poets, it has mostly been the other way around— average intelligence, average or below-average literacy, and enormous radicalism. The radicalism often seems, by comparison with Pound or Auden or Berryman or Lowell, naïve.

Lowell or Auden could control a tone of insolence like

Berryman's in "The Lay of Ike," but not many other poets today have the cultural premises to make it hold. The poem posits an underlying patriotism, the regularly-invoked patriotism of John Adams, perhaps. (It follows the Song called "Of 1828" which quotes Adams's dying words.) It rests on an historical mannerliness that makes its goosing of a president *serious*. It is funny but it's no joke. We are made aware of a heritage that President Eisenhower is being insulted for *not* being aware of. It is a vulgar, telling statement of expectation from one of the last of the unreconstructed patriots.

On the Sunday morning at the end of that weekend at Goddard there was an easy discussion among poets and student poets—I think it was billed as a symposium—in the living room of the guesthouse we had stayed in. Berryman was in good form, despite the fact that for four days he had been without the sedative (my quiet pills, he called them) he took during those last months when he was not drinking. He was wonderfully attentive, in the way I had seen him in the classroom at Bread Loaf. The talk was set in motion by Paul Nelson, the poet who teaches at Goddard. His quiet good sense set an unpretentious tone for an event that might well have become competitive. Of the poets who had been there for the weekend I think only Galway Kinnell had left before this final session. I remember that Louise Glück, Michael Dennis Browne, James Tate, Barry Goldensen, Marvin Bell, Geof Hewitt, and Charles Simic were still there.

After Nelson had thanked the poets, he turned the discussion over to Berryman, who surprised me by introducing me. I was not an invited member of the weekend but John's guest. One of the things he said about me was that I understood Frost better than anyone else and had survived him, the way he (Berryman) understood and had survived Yeats. I said a poem I knew by heart and read one out of my journal. He asked for one I had written about Frost, but it simply would not come to me and I petered out after a few lines. Then John said, "Why doesn't everyone in the gathering of poets say what he thinks he has done best?" It was a good half hour or so then, unusual human warmth came of that quite characteristic act on the part of a man who is often described as arrogant. The poets were completely open with one another, modest before their calling with a modesty that John had laid on us.

At the end a student, a young woman, read a strong, not altogether controlled surrealist poem, and John responded. He spoke about breakthrough works, and said that the first section of his "Homage to Mistress Bradstreet" had been a kind of "first best" for him—too long, but exciting as a first. He called it a "crisis poem." It was a phrase he had used earlier in the weekend, talking in wide generalizations about the "Dream Songs." The first 384 are about the death of his father, he said, and number 385 is about the illegitimate pregnancy of his daughter (an infant in arms at Thanksgiving, 1962, when the poem can be dated). "I am interested only in people in crisis," he said. "When I finish one, I enter on another." (I incline to agree with a student of his work, Deborah Melone, who was present at the Sunday morning meeting, that in this reference to the final Dream Song, as often in talking about his poems, he was trying on a new meaning that had suggested itself to him, or in this case been suggested to him, after the fact. When the poem was written, I think, the opening words—"My daughter's heavier"—referred to the process of growth, suggesting the process of mortality.)

I think now that the most important persuasion we shared— I a virtually unread, instinctive, gregarious man, Berryman one of the most learned, intellectual, and lonely men I've known—was a view about people in crisis. It amounts to a qualified optimism, in his case ultimately a Christian optimism, about crisis as a medium of grace, if an agnostic can put it that way. We both believed that there is an appropriate response to anything that befalls a human being, and that the game is to find and present that response.

Robert Frost's "The Draft Horse," a poem John asked me to say that morning at Goddard (he knew I had it by heart, as I didn't have my poem about Frost), is a poem about the mystery of response to crisis, implying I think that the response of love can render evil impotent. Berryman makes a response to it ("Lines to Mr. Frost") in his final collection, lines from one poet at rest, now, to another, concluding, "I was almost ready to hear you from the grave with these passionate grave last words, and frankly Sir you fill me with joy."

The night before I picked him up at Hartford, he had endured a crisis in his hotel there and had written, or anyhow started writing, the astonishing religious poem called "The Facts & Issues." It begins:

> I really believe He's here all over this room
> in a motor hotel in Wallace Stevens' town.

It contains the lines about his friends quoted first in this reminiscence. It ends with the baffling spectacle of a man fending off torrents of a grace that has become unbearable. It is an heroic response to that crisis, as I think his death was too.

As we drove toward Vermont the next afternoon he told me that he had telephoned his wife that night and asked her (at 4 A.M. again) to tell him "of any act of pure and costly giving" in his life. "I can't stand any more luck, I can't take any more. Neither heaven nor hell—rest, when it's over." I am a bad journalist and an agnostic besides, but I wrote that down that night, in Woodstock, and pray now that it is so for him.

The Lasting Voice

As I put together these, my profoundly felt if not profoundly original remarks about Randall Jarrell, I listened several times to a recording of his. Perhaps we still underestimate the importance of this innovation in the preservation of poetry. The poets' voices which began to be recorded in our century will retain for future readers rhythms and tones which have died with all previous poets. These sounds are surely subordinate in importance to that permanent voice which is written into the words and is proof against declamation by actors, recitation by school children, and impersonation by school teachers and other poets. Nevertheless the living voice may have contributed to the contemporary understanding of a poet and perhaps to the real voice, as that voice was first established among contemporaries and intimates of the poet.

At the memorial service held at Yale University for Randall Jarrell the February after his death, for example, the voices of two of his friends and contemporaries must have struck most hearers as much as they did me. Robert Lowell's readings carry always a slight tone of complaint, as though he would make some disappointment heard beyond that of man's tragic predicament. This disappointment, half modest, half the reverse, seems to express: although I am the man of remarkable vision who has seen and said this, am I not sadly unremarkable? John Berryman's voice, more sharply than his poems, conveys continuously astonishment and intermittently outrage: is this predicament to be believed or to be borne? To

In *Randall Jarrell 1914–1965,* edited by Robert Lowell, Peter Taylor, and Robert Penn Warren (Farrar, Straus & Giroux, 1965).

have heard either of these men read is to learn some final secrets about the enduring voice on the page and the enduring vision of the man.

The vision of a serious artist is a very individual matter. Perhaps the most important thing he has to learn is, what am I clairvoyant about, what do I see *into* that other people simply see? The minor artist is, by comparison, a beachcomber. He lives off the discovery of novel beauties and horrors; he sees them *first,* but he sees them with the flat eyes of just anybody. Novelty in this sense is nothing to the serious artist, or worse than nothing, a temptation to desert his individual vision. We can't imagine Wallace Stevens trying to penetrate the complacencies of an oven bird, or Frost the complacencies of a peignoir. Artists like that know who they are and what they can see into.

Randall Jarrell's progress, volume by volume, seems to have been toward greater awareness of what he could call his own. For many years he was clearly one of our best poets, in the company of Wilbur, Berryman, Roethke, and Lowell, but he wasn't perfectly sure what to do with his restless gift. He wrote a number of brittle, chilly poems that detach themselves from life with an irresponsible irony—poems like "The State," "Sears Roebuck," and "Variations"—which may be all right as poems but never seem to be quite Jarrell. At the same time he was consistently producing marvelous, deep-running dramatic poems that from the first were stamped with his voice and his eye for subjective imagery: "Second Air Force," "Seele im Raum," "The End of the Rainbow."

The recognition of his especial vision, which was complete with his fine last book, *The Lost World,* involved two things, though perhaps they were a single act: abandoning a timid, mechanical skepticism and embracing a wide human involvement. The accomplishment of these seems to have confirmed another fact: his gift was essentially dramatic, like Browning's.

Comparing poems that span a number of years, we can see his dramatic talent grow brighter as though controlled by a rheostat. He returns to characters, images, even to lines. "A Hunt in the Black Forest" in *The Lost World* opens with the same lines that had opened, seventeen years before in *Losses,*

"The Child of Courts." And the returns to apparently autobiographical events of childhood are even more striking. There are things a man goes over and over until he gets them right.

Take a character that Jarrell finds in many guises, the woman whose growing old is an inexplicable and brutal mystery to her. Three poems on this theme, spaced over a number of years, conclude as follows:

> But it's not *right.*
> If just living can do this,
> Living is more dangerous than anything:
>
> It is terrible to be alive.
>
> ("The Face")

> Vulture,
> When you come for the white rat that the foxes left,
> Take off the red helmet of your head, the black
> Wings that have shadowed me, and step to me as man:
> The wild brother at whose feet the white wolves fawn,
> To whose hand of power the great lioness
> Stalks, purring. . . .
> You know what I was,
> You see what I am: change me, change me!
> ("The Woman at the Washington Zoo")

> I am afraid, this morning, of my face.
> It looks at me
> From the rear-view mirror, with the eyes I hate,
> The smile I hate. Its plain, lined look
> Of gray discovery
> Repeats to me: "You're old." That's all, I'm old.
>
> And yet I'm afraid, as I was at the funeral
> I went to yesterday.
> My friend's cold made-up face, granite among its flowers,
> Her undressed, operated-on, dressed body
> Were my face and body.
> As I think of her I hear her telling me
>
> How young I seem; I *am* exceptional;
> I think of all I have.
> But really no one is exceptional,

No one has anything, I'm anybody,
I stand beside my grave
Confused with my life, that is commonplace and solitary.
                                                    ("Next Day")

Granted that some of the differences come from the sub-
jects' differences: the woman in "The Face" seems to have an
aristocratic beauty, and her epigraph identifies her with the
Marschallin in *Der Rosenkavalier;* the woman at the zoo seems
to be an unmarried office worker; the woman in the final
passage, the conclusion of the opening poem in *The Lost World,*
is a suburban wife. (Of the woman in the Washington Zoo,
Jarrell wrote that she is "a distant relation of women I have
written about before, in "The End of the Rainbow" and "Cin-
derella" and "Seele im Raum.") But the final passage above is,
in the first place, free of the glamour of violence. It makes its
point, it involves us, without a Marschallin on the one hand or
a vulture on the other. Dailiness has been seen as its drama,
rather than rank or sexuality. ("Vulture is a euphemism," Jar-
rell wrote about this.) And the attitude of the poet in "Next
Day" seems therefore a great deal more compassionate. In-
stead of crying, *beauty! horror!* he seems to be saying, *life, life,*
with a vision that elevates that remark to wisdom—that is to
say, with a kind of wondering acceptance. He says this explic-
itly in the poem called "Well Water":

> What a girl called "the dailiness of life"
> (Adding an errand to your errand. Saying,
> "Since you're up . . ." Making you a means to
> A means to a means to) is well water
> Pumped from an old well at the bottom of the world.
> The pump you pump the water from is rusty
> And hard to move and absurd, a squirrel-wheel
> A sick squirrel turns slowly, through the sunny
> Inexorable hours. And yet sometimes
> The wheel turns of its own weight, the rusty
> Pump pumps over your sweating face the clear
> Water, cold, so cold! you cup your hands
> And gulp from them the dailiness of life.

The irony in this poem, and in most of the poems in the last book, turns as much toward himself as it turns outward, and adds to the compassion which inflects his true voice. Some of his reputation, a part I still cannot applaud, came from an acid humor which he turned on people and things from whom he withheld sympathy. He could be very funny under these circumstances, if you shared his unsympathy, but he never wrote as skillfully then as he did in appreciation.

Listening now to his early reading of "Lady Bates," an early poem, is a painful experience. So much feeling and understanding beyond what is on the page emerges from his delivery. "These are the bones of stories, and we shiver at them," he wrote about two poems by Blake and Stephen Crane. The voice of all his best poems is that of a storyteller almost too deeply involved to speak. The stories themselves, though, lie exactly right for his voice, as they say of certain songs for certain singers.

A man of his intellectual brilliance must have known better than most of us the consequences of such wide and unguarded sympathy. Many of the stresses of his life must have come from checking, and from failing to check, a great generosity of heart. The poems he left behind seem to me to speak in the most compassionate voice of any of his generation. What you would hear if you stood outside a door and could not make out the words the voice was saying (*the sound of sense,* Frost called this) might be what St. Irene's hands convey in "The Old and the New Masters":

> Revealing, accepting, what she does not understand.
> Her hands say: "Lo! Behold!"

With this voice he was able to say beautiful, tentative things no one else could say.

Robert Lowell at the Opera

The art of opera is so much its own kind, *sui generis*, that when we say something else is operatic the comparison is usually a deliberately strained one, often suggesting that both opera and the thing likened to it are ridiculous. To speak of a political aria by Bella Abzug is to make a stereoscopic metaphor, merging one image of fustian with another.

Robert Lowell's work is operatic in a literal and serious sense. His characters are more broadly and strongly delineated than in most modern poetry. His originality lies not in the rejection of the large inherited conventions but in their modification. And his plots are redeemed from melodrama by gorgeous language much as the plots of many operas are raised by music.

In a time without much sense of history, Robert Lowell's work is conspicuous for its vivid and personal historical fantasies. The characters of Cleopatra and Thomas More, of Joinville and Anne Boleyn, are as visual as dreams, in his poems. Moral and political troubles seem disturbingly like our own, in a way that suggests that history is a continuum: what is beautiful or admirable has always been brief and perilous, what is wrong with men and women has always been wrong.

Dante may have been the model for his method of rendering character: a spotlight thrown on a crucial moment. Christopher Marlowe (in Lowell's *History*), "hurled from England to his companion shades," says: "Tragedy is to die for that vacant parsonage, Posterity; my plays are stamped in bronze, my life in tabloid." (History itself is an anachronism in Lowell's work:

Musical Newsletter 7, no. 4 (Fall 1977).

we cannot help imposing present values on it—we have no others—and when we read it we conjure it out of its context and into the present.)

The things his characters say and their gestures and stances are operatic, then. Lowell himself had a feeling for opera and a special if limited understanding of it, not unlike my own. This memoir springs from a friendship which began when his old friend and editor Robert Giroux introduced us at the opera in 1955.

In March 1960 the Ford Foundation awarded fellowships to eleven poets and fiction writers and arranged for each writer to be associated with a theater or opera company. "The intention of the program," W. McNeil Lowry wrote for the Foundation, "is to bring established writers in non-dramatic forms into formal association with the theater and, by acquainting them with stage problems and the requirements of dramatic writing, ultimately to improve the quality of plays and scripts available to American directors, actors and producers." Robert Lowell and I, at our own request, were accredited to the New York City and Metropolitan Opera Companies and went to New York in the fall of 1960.

The New York City Opera season opened on September 29 with new productions of Monteverdi's *Orfeo* and Dallapiccola's *The Prisoner*. Starting in mid-September we spent many hours at the City Center at rehearsals of those two remarkable and, to us, unfamiliar works. Julius Rudel was immediately accommodating and accessible, and Lowell and I could talk to singers, musicians, and directors during lulls in the rehearsals. (I don't think we ever talked to Stokowski, who conducted the double bill, though I remember his strong presence as the works were assembled.)

The Prisoner, a marvel of twelve-tone theater, was sung in an undistinguished translation, and during the first week it occurred to Lowell and me that we might touch up some of the unhappier lines before the opening performance. I recently turned up a page of recitative which seems to have been an abortive collaboration, the first few words in Lowell's curious printed lettering. But we never satisfied even ourselves, and didn't pass our effort along.

Chiefly we played a passive but attentive role, talking opera with one another and with the citizens of this new backstage world. Gérard Souzay, who sang *Orfeo*, was particularly articulate about the opera, a work whose appearance in 1607 seems now altogether miraculous, the invention of opera. The important role that the ballet played in that production perhaps started Lowell on what became another intense interest for him that winter.

We stayed with the company during the preparation of Werner Egk's *The Inspector General*, which was conducted by the composer and imaginatively directed by William Ball. By the time it opened on October 19th, we were already attending rehearsals at the Met.

Our first interview with Rudolf Bing made it clear that we would be on shiftier ground at the Metropolitan Opera House. We were received, after several days of negotiation, about as unpretentiously as into the Oval Office, and Mr. Bing that morning showed the easy self-effacement of Richard Nixon and the quick intelligence of his successor. After assuring himself that we represented the Ford Foundation in no useful way, he seemed puzzled about what to do with us. He proposed that we should go to school: his assistant, John Gutman, offered an introductory course in opera at Columbia which we could attend. "We are already professionals in our work, Mr. Bing," Lowell said. "We're here to see how opera is produced." In the end, we were given house-passes, treated with mild distrust by the management, but befriended where it mattered, by the singers and other professionals we wanted to talk to. I found it bracing to be greeted occasionally as "Mr. Lowell" by the General Manager himself.

At the Met we followed for many days the preparation of Gluck's *Alcestis* (also sung in a regrettable translation), the production that belatedly brought Eileen Farrell into the company. Conducted by Erich Leinsdorf, it was as exciting a work to see come to life as *Orfeo* had been.

We attended several rehearsals of a revived production of *Arabella*. It was at one of these I became aware of how much more ponderous was the machinery of the Met than that of the City Opera. Rehearsals were constantly interrupted for trivial details of staging or acting, while a full cast in costume, and the orchestra and conductor, were standing idle.

Our passes admitted us to performances, and we could stand along the south wall of the orchestra, where some of the younger singers sometimes leaned. I was backstage the night Leontyne Price made her debut in *Trovatore*. My friend Helen Vanni, who was singing Inez, introduced me. With her extraordinary composure, Price asked me, a few moments before her first cue, what was a poet attached to the company for?

Lowell was never as interested in what was going on at the Met, except for meeting some of his favorite singers and conductors, as he had been in the early weeks at the City Center where Rudel had seen to it that he was recognized as a fellow artist. And it was not an exciting season. Harold Schonberg wrote of the Met that year:

> First, the repertory. It is, on the whole, dull and lopsided. . . . Its disdain of the modern school is epochal. . . . The way the Metropolitan is going, it is ceasing to be a part of the intellectual life of the city.

Lowell was quicker to sense that than I was, or to mind it. After the first six weeks he continued to attend occasional performances. But he was working on poems. The translation of *Phaedre* he had made the summer before had led him into a run of lyric translations that were to become *Imitations;* and in late winter he had one of his recurrent breakdowns.

Of an intended collaboration between us, he has given this account:

> I was asked by Eric Bentley to translate Racine's *Phaedre* for a classic theater anthology he was editing, and I spent a summer doing that. It was something I had always wanted to do and the experience stuck in my mind. Then I received a grant to go to opera rehearsals at the Met. I went with my friend, the poet William Meredith, who is also an opera expert, and we decided we would make a libretto out of Melville's "Benito Cereno." When I finally left New York in the middle of the summer to do my version of "Benito," I found I had finished it as a play before he had started on our operatic collaboration.

In addition to hearing more opera in a short period of time than he had probably ever heard before, Lowell went to the ballet a good deal that winter. He and I had renewed our friendships with Lincoln Kirstein, and sometimes went to the New York City Ballet with him, sometimes went to his house afterwards to join him for talk about that other great Romantic extravagance of art. Lowell's feeling for ballet was direct and amateur. He *believed* the drama that was being danced, as he (and I) believed the drama that was being sung at the opera houses. In this sense, I think he apprehended opera historically, as in its own time, rather than with the distance that it is usually understood today.

To be able to believe in Bellini's *Norma* or Rossini's *Mosè in Egitto* as their contemporary audiences believed requires a great historical sense, or a great naiveté, or perhaps both. There is evidence that these operas were taken perfectly seriously as drama, in their own day. Serious artists and critics compared them to Greek drama. Stendhal wrote of the first performance of *Mosè:*

> Benedetti, who sang the part of Moses, appeared in a simple and sublime costume, the model for which he had taken from the statue by Michelangelo in S. Pietro in Vincoli in Rome. Hardly had he addressed twenty words to the Eternal God when my mind ceased making critical comments: in him I no longer saw a charlatan who changed staffs into serpents, but a great man, a minister of the Omnipotent, who made a vile tyrant tremble on his throne. I still remember the effect his words made on me: "Eterno, immenso, incomprensibil Dio!" This entrance of Moses reminded me of all that is most lofty in Haydn.

A mind which cannot "cease making critical comments" in the face of stylized artifice is unlikely to find opera or ballet congenial forms today. A lot of distortion occurs in modern operatic production when attempts are made to deny essential stylization. Perhaps the worst of Rudolf Bing's doctrinal errors—seen in the famous *Barber of Seville* which Cyril Ritchard directed—was his belief that it is possible to stage opera so that people who don't like opera will think they are at the theater, or better, at the music hall.

Lowell's mind "ceased making critical comments" in the most generous and enlightened way, by instinctively and knowingly returning to the responses which a work of art first invited. This kind of insight he brought also to historical events and characters, an acceptance on their own terms.

I think he found the fantasy which sustains opera, and particularly early nineteenth-century Italian opera, deeply congenial. He seems to have retained none of his mentor Eliot's prejudice against the Romantic movement. In a remarkable identification with Wordsworth—remarkable among other reasons because Lowell was so intellectual a man—he wrote to me after putting together his *Selected Poems*, "I felt in reading my *Selected*, continuously, in a way for the first time, that all I have written is a stream of autobiography, sometimes intimate, often distant, yet always personal, a small continuous Prelude."

Lowell never wrote a libretto. It might be possible to show that the three plays he finished the following year and yoked under the title *The Old Glory*, have operatic conventions. But I think this would be using a false metaphor, like speaking of the music of poetry, and I prefer to hold the larger claim I made at the start of this piece, that Lowell's poetry itself suggests the scale and strategy of opera. His interest in drama was already evident in his remark about *Phaedre*. A few years later he would adapt Aeschylus's *Prometheus Bound* as freely as he had dealt with Melville and Hawthorne—alchemies of a mind at home with everything except boundaries.

I believe that like me he could do little more than follow a score, as far as a technical understanding of opera was concerned. But it was an art he loved and understood as an artist. There were resonances. In the poem "Napoleon" in his volume *History* we read these lines of a man who knew the sweet addiction of it:

> three million soldiers dead,
> grand opera fixed like morphine in their veins.

Remembering Robert Lowell

I climbed the several flights of stairs to the pair of rooms at the top of Dunster House, at Harvard, where he stayed last spring when he was teaching there. He was expecting me, I was ready for the strong infusion of mind and energy that at first always seemed overwhelming, yet both of us were glad and shy for the first moments. "Our not getting together yearly is unnatural, isn't it?" he'd written me. We went into the little sitting room, bleak with institutional furniture and (this happened wherever he alighted for more than a day) spread with papers and books.

I hadn't heard much about the new book, which he showed me some revised and written-over poems from—I remember especially the "Ulysses and Circe" series. Nor about Caroline's plans—their plans, he told me, though it turned out that they had separate plans—to sell the house in Kent and move to a rather grand house in Ireland where they would take apartments. (When I saw her in New York two months later, she showed me a picture of the beautiful Palladian house. It bore out Cal's remark that it was a slightly reduced version of Versailles. But they were not to live there together.) What heavy changes were occurring in the marriage he didn't tell me. We were not suddenly that intimate, after almost two years; the friendship had suffered disuse, and that matter was private.

Lowell was sometimes reticent about his private life, in conversation, however confessional he became when he talked to himself in poems. I think the poems were often spoken primarily to himself, if intended for us. This accounts for some

Yale Lit. 147, no. 1 (1977–78).

of their uncommunicativeness: things he needn't say to himself, to locate a poem, are left puzzlingly unsaid for the reader, who needs them.

And he told me about his recent hospitalization. What I recall him saying was that he had gone to McLean's in February for tests in preparation for a new treatment—perhaps a less drastic treatment than the lithium he'd been taking for a long time to dampen out the manic-depressive cycles—and that the routine electro-cardiogram had shown that he had recently suffered a mild heart attack. He told me, as a comic scenario, how he had been taken by emergency procedures from McLean's to the Massachusetts General Hospital—I think I recall these, to me, unknown places right—from which he had been released only a few days before this. When I asked him about taking care of himself—the flights of stairs here, the cigarettes he was smoking as always since I'd known him—he said he was getting well, was allowed to do all the things he was doing. I said that in Japan he would be designated an Important Cultural Property and looked after. I think what he replied was, joking, that the experience had made him feel mortal.

I liked the new poems, was struck with their dramatic and narrative quality after the long expository years of *Notebook* poems, and told him I found them more accessible. It was at this point, shortly before we went out for dinner, that I remember saying (more in the spirit of Rod McKuen than of James Joyce) that I thought his language was moving nearer to language of the tribe. I have always felt that his poems made severer demands on their readers than they needed to, have always felt that many modern poets neglect the vulgar energy of speech for a literary language of their own. My remark was intended as praise, then, was in a context of praise, and as far as I remember he seemed to understand it so, though his poem would suggest something more ambivalent on one or both sides.

In our relationship as writers (and he made me think of myself as a writer, a thing I normally avoid), the role I had assumed was to show him, frequently by asking questions, places where his poems were unclear: where the reader was not told clearly what the poem was saying (rather than what it meant). We had been together in Madrid in 1969 when the proofs of the first *Notebook* arrived from the publisher. He made a number of last-minute changes, many of them to clarify passages I had convinced him were not clear, not located in the poem as they were in his experience. It was against a long background of comments like that, that I spoke last March about the clarity of *Day by Day*.

It was a very rainy evening. We walked down the stairs, and from almost the bottom he went back up to his rooms to get an umbrella. Then we went through the courtyard and indoors again through a kind of porter's lodge and out across the yard to my car. We drove across the Charles and down Marlborough Street, past the house where I first stayed with Elizabeth Hardwick and him more than twenty years before, to the Athens-Olympia, a Greek restaurant I like—the only restaurant I know in Boston, in fact—though whether it was his choice or mine I can't remember. It is "on the edge of Boston's Combat Zone," as he says in "Morning after Dining with a Friend." Of that dinner, I remember a few other things, and a few things differently, from the poem's memory.

The restaurant was almost deserted on a rainy Sunday night. We sat in a booth along the front wall of the front dining room. When I came back from the men's room, across the long, empty space of half-light, he said, "It seems strange to see you with white hair. And I (all self-deception, convinced at this writing that I have only a few gray hairs at the temples and perhaps in the scraggly rear of my head) said something about the lighting being deceptive. He was thinking, as I determinedly was not, of the years that had passed since I was thirty-six.

> I met you first at the old Met Opera Club,
> shy, correct, in uniform,
> your regulation on active duty
> substitute for black-tie—
>
> Poet and aviator
> at 36,
> the eternal autumn of youth.

That image has gained body;
yet shrinks back this morning
to its greener Platonic shade,
the man of iron—

not drinking, terrified
of losing your mind. . . .
turning to me, calm
by a triumph of impersonation:

"If you could come a little nearer
the language of the tribe."

When we talked about Frost, what I remember saying was not

"I think Frost liked me better
but found you more amusing."

but "I think Frost found you more interesting." Amusing is
not a weighty word in my vocabulary, not a praise word, cer-
tainly not a word adequate to the felt disturbance of heart,
dazzle of mind, that one experienced in Lowell's company,
even in the most intimate and joking of his moments. He was
a very funny man, a great mimic, a playful father, but I never
thought of this profound gaity so archly as to call it amusing.

I write these remarks as if answering a letter from a dead
man whom I loved, because I didn't see the poem I've quoted
until after his death. The things I want to tell my side of are
trivial, measured against the honor of the undedicated poem,
the honor of his friendship. But I meant to say to him that
night that I envied him that he could interest Frost more than
I could have hoped to. I meant also to say that I was glad that
the new poems seemed nearer to the density and energy of
common verbal experience.

What may have happened overnight—

Why have I twisted your kind words
and tortured myself till morning?

the poem asks—what may have happened overnight is that
my remark phrased itself as a question, and that he attributed

that question about his language to me, who had asked him so many.

He inscribed a copy of his *Selected Poems* before I left him that night in his rooms. "One's books moving n . . .", he wrote and then struck that out and wrote instead "One's language moving nearer the language. . . ." Stanley Kunitz has recently spoken of how naturally Lowell spoke of friendship as love. The dedication (a phrase still undeciphered) is signed, "Love, Cal."

Before I saw "Morning after Dining with a Friend," but after I had pondered the inscription, I wrote a poem in his memory containing the line:

Your language moved slowly towards our language.

He and the English language were capable of moving one another perceptibly, by attraction, both being of a certain amplitude.

Remembering Robert Lowell

The message you brought back again and again
from the dark brink had the glitter of truth.
From the beginning, you told it as memoir:
even though you didn't cause it,
the memoirs said of the trouble they recounted,
it was always your familiar when it came.

Your language moved slowly towards our language
until we saw that we were all immigrants—
had perhaps been shipped as convicts—
from the land of your reluctant indictment,
a land of our consent, if not of our doing.

It was your jokes and stories, when you were alive,
the wry imitations and the bad boy's laugh,
that roped us from the brink you led us to.
We will miss that laughter, left to the glittering poems,
the raw gist of things.

To punish the bearer of evil tidings
it is our custom to ask his blessing.
This you gave. It dawns on each of us separately now
what this entails.

II

On Poetry

Reasons for Poetry

The Mexican poet José Emilio Pacheco, in a poem called "Dissertation on Poetic Propriety," asks for "a new definition . . . a name, some term or other . . . to avoid the astonishment and rages of those who say, so reasonably, looking at a poem: 'Now this is not poetry.' " I too want to argue for a broader definition of poetry, a definition which will increase our sense of the multitudes that poetry contains. For those of us who care about poetry in this time of widely diverging definitions are apt to be consciously limited in our tastes, and churlish in our distastes. We often have more precise ideas, based on these distastes, about what poetry is not than about what it is.

If I cannot come up with the new definition Pacheco asks for, what I say is at least intended to turn aside the easy negative response in myself and in others to poems which are not immediately congenial. For whenever we say, "Now this is not poetry," we are adding to the disuse of all poetry.

Perhaps the most useful definition, in fact, would begin with a statement about expectation: the expectation with which a reader engages a poem, and the reasons for which a poet may have undertaken the poem, and the possible discrepancy between these two. We have all had the experience of fighting a work of art because it was not doing what we were asking of it. John Ashbery said in an interview: "My feeling is that a poem that communicates something that's already known to the reader is not really communicating anything to him and in fact shows a lack of respect for him." Since what is

---

Poetry Consultant's Annual Address, delivered at the Library of Congress, May 7, 1979. First published by the Library of Congress, 1982.

communicated in a work of art is also how it is communicated, a false expectation is almost certain to produce a false reading. And often we confirm this by the happy surprise that comes when a work we had been defeated by suddenly opens itself to us—we find that it performs very well the job of work which was its reason, once we stop asking it to perform some other service which was no part of its intention.

A word here about *liking* a poem. This should of course be our primary objective and motive. But to like is a function of the critical intelligence, as this passage by W. H. Auden makes clear:

> As readers, we remain in the nursery stage as long as we cannot distinguish between taste and judgment, so long, that is, as the only possible verdicts we can pass on a book are two: this I like, this I don't like.

He goes on with the lovely, schoolmasterly, and abashing accuracy of an Audenism:

> For an adult reader, the possible verdicts are five: I can see this is good and I like it; I can see this is good but I don't like it; I can see this is good and, though at present I don't like it, I believe that with perseverance I shall come to like it; I can see this is trash but I like it; I can see this is trash and I don't like it.

My argument is that we should use the third option as often as possible, when the first response is not spontaneous with us. When we can't say of a poem, especially of a poem that comes recommended, I can see this is good and I like it, we owe it to ourselves and the poem to try to say, I can see this is good, and though at present I don't like it, I believe that with perseverance, et cetera.

Poems seem to come into being for various and distinct reasons. These vary from poem to poem and from poet to poet. The reason for a poem is apt to be one of the revelations attendant on its making. No surprise in the writer, no surprise in the reader, Frost said. The reason for a new poem is, in some essential, a new reason. This is why poets, in the large Greek sense of *makers,* are crucial to a culture. They respond newly, but in the familiar tribal experience of language, to what new thing befalls the tribe. I shall have some comments to make here about three generic reasons for which poems seem to come into being, but even within these genera, the occasion of a poem is always a new thing under the sun.

And poets don't respond as one, they respond in character, with various intuition, to the new experience. What each maker makes is poetry, but why he makes it, his reason, is his unique intuition. The reason determines the proper mode of apprehension. It is part of the purpose of every poem to surprise us with our own capacity for change, for a totally new response. For example, David Wagoner's lines called aggressively, "This Is a Wonderful Poem":

> Come at it carefully, don't trust it, that isn't its right name,
> It's wearing stolen rags, it's never been washed, its breath
> Would look moss-green if it were really breathing,
> It won't get out of the way, it stares at you
> Out of eyes burnt gray as the sidewalk,
> Its skin is overcast with colorless dirt,
> It has no distinguishing marks, no I. D. cards,
> It wants something of yours but hasn't decided
> Whether to ask for it or just take it,
> There are no policemen, no friendly neighbors,
> No peacekeeping busybodies to yell for, only this
> Thing standing between you and the place you were headed,
> You have about thirty seconds to get past it, around it,
> Or simply to back away and try to forget it,
> It won't take no for an answer: try hitting it first
> And you'll learn what's trembling in its torn pocket.
> Now, what do you want to do about it?

The resilience such a poem asks of us is a reader's first responsibility. To assume one knows what a poem is going to do is (to turn John Ashbery's statement around) to show a lack of respect for it. I think it is chiefly a lack of resilience that has kept the poetry public so small in our country, and has divided what public there is into dozens of hostile sects. We say of our own chosen poetry—Olsen or Frost, Lowell or Bly—the poetry whose reasons strike us as reasonable, "Now this is poetry," and then generally, of everything else, loudly, airily and with great conviction, "and this is not." Criticism, which is at its most perceptive when most appreciative, is thus often *narrowly* appreciative. It divides and rules and does little to promulgate the astonishment, the larger force of poetry.

And it is very easy to reject poems whose reasons do not declare or recommend themselves to us. Take an extreme mode of recent poetry which Robert Pinsky has described in *The Situation of Poetry*. This school, he says, has "a prevalent diction or manner" which embodies, "in language, a host of reservations about language, human reason, and their holds on life." He quotes a poem by W. S. Merwin and says of it: "It moves in a resolutely elliptical way from image to atomistic image, finally reaching a kind of generalization-against generalizing in the line:

> Today belongs to few and tomorrow to no one."

Pinsky concludes: "This poem presents a style well suited to a certain deeply skeptical or limiting vision of the poetic imagination and its place in the world."

To appreciate a poem conceived in these terms—conceived for what many readers would consider non-reasons—is not easy for most of us. What kind of poem harbors "a host of reservations about language, human reason, and their holds on life," and with a "deeply skeptical or limiting vision of the poetic imagination and its place in the world"? *Aha!* says the part of our mind that waits with a club for *what is not a poem*. How can anything call itself a poem if it mistrusts language and the power of the poetic imagination? Is not all mystery made lucid to the poetic imagination, and precisely in language? But the often ill-advised left side of the brain is wrong to thus object. Let us ask it to consider a poem whose last line proclaims this heresy, whose last line in fact is, "There are limits to imagination." This is Robert Hass's beautiful "Heroic Simile." It purports to be a simile about how a soldier falls in a certain Japanese movie, and it likens him chiefly to a great pine tree, an image which does not appear in the movie:

Heroic Simile

When the swordsman fell in Kurosawa's *Seven Samurai*
in the gray rain,
in Cinemascope and the Tokugawa dynasty,
he fell straight as a pine, he fell
as Ajax fell in Homer
in chanted dactyls and the tree was so huge
the woodsman returned for two days
to that lucky place before he was done with the sawing
and on the third day he brought his uncle.

They stacked logs in the resinous air,
hacking the small limbs off,
tying those bundles separately.
The slabs near the root
were quartered and still they were awkwardly large;
the logs from midtree they halved:
ten bundles and four great piles of fragrant wood,
moons and quarter moons and half moons
ridged by the saw's tooth.

The woodsman and the old man his uncle
are standing in midforest
on a floor of pine silt and spring mud.
They have stopped working
because they are tired and because
I have imagined no pack animal
or primitive wagon. They are too canny
to call in neighbors and come home
with a few logs after three days' work.
They are waiting for me to do something
or for the overseer of the Great Lord
to come and arrest them.

How patient they are!
The old man smokes a pipe and spits.
The young man is thinking he would be rich
if he were already rich and had a mule.
Ten days of hauling
and on the seventh day they'll probably
be caught, go home empty-handed
or worse. I don't know
whether they're Japanese or Mycenaean

and there's nothing I can do.
The path from here to that village
is not translated. A hero, dying,
gives off stillness to the air.
A man and a woman walk from the movies
to the house in the silence of separate fidelities.
There are limits to imagination.

At one critical point in the narrative—and the simile is offered as a story—the poet heightens the mystery of metamorphosis by dramatizing the process itself:

They have stopped working
because they are tired and because
I have imagined no pack animal
or primitive wagon . . .
They are waiting for me to do something
or for the overseer of the Great Lord
to come and arrest them . . .

I don't know
whether they're Japanese or Mycenaean
and there's nothing I can do.

We are asked to believe that the poem takes place at the limits of imagination, where the poet's debilitating reluctances threaten to overpower his fancy and drag it back into the territory of the literal. And the poem shows us, by exhibiting its own process, how the energy is to be found, in the process of simile itself, to mix modes and times and feelings in ways that are disturbing and mysterious and, for our souls' sakes, necessary.

Here I want to posit three roles a poem may take, and to suggest that one of these roles accounts for the stance a poem takes. I offer these three stances not to head off the proper surprise of a new poem but as an exercise in resilience, the way you might strengthen your eyesight by looking at objects near, middling, and far in regular succession. I think of them as three *reasons* for poetry, identifiable genetically with the DNA impulse which starts a poem growing. The reason behind a poem shapes its growth and determines the way it is delivered. To stretch the metaphor further, it determines how the poem is to be picked up and spanked into breath by the reader.

If every poem is new, it is also associated in its own mind, and ideally in the reader's, with other poems of its species. Poems hold one another in place in our minds, Robert Frost said, the way the stars hold one another in place in the firmament.

The three roles I envision are these:

1. The poet as dissident. Underlying poems conceived by the poet as dissident is a social criticism, whether of a tyranny, like George III's or Stalin's, of an abuse, like nuclear pollution, or of a system, like capitalism. As an activist poet, the dissident is likely to be formally radical, since the large metaphor of his work is revolution, but not necessarily.

2. The poet as apologist. Underlying poems conceived by the poet as apologist is acceptance or approval of the human and social predicament of his tribe. However much the poem may focus on errors or imperfections in its subject, there is implied an order or decorum in the model. Often the poem's mode is praise, overt or implicit, of the specific subject or of the human condition. Every work of art, the Christian apologist W. H. Auden said, is by its formal nature a gesture of astonishment at that greatest of miracles, the principle of order in the universe. The poet as apologist is apt to have a pronounced sense of form, but not necessarily.

3. The third and commonest stance of the poet is the poet as solitary. While the poem by the poet as solitary will sometimes take the stance of talking to itself, more often it speaks from the poet as individual to the reader as another individual, and intends to establish a limited, intense agreement of feeling. There is no implicit agreement about social needs or predicaments. Such solitary experiences, and they make up most of lyric poetry, carry on their backs the world they are concerned with, like itinerant puppet-shows. They create a momentary event where the poet and the reader dwell together in some mutual astonishment of words. The best teacher I ever had told us a lyric poem can only say one of three things. It can say, "Oh, the beauty of it" or "Oh, the pity of it," or it can say, "Oh."

This is a crude trinity, and if useful at all, useful at the elementary level of detecting and dispelling false expectation. I will rehearse the three roles with some examples.

If a poet is committed to an overriding social grievance, as currently some of the best European, Latin American, and United States minority writers are, the poem is best read as a kind of ceremonial rite, with a specific purpose. A dissident poem aspires to be an effective ritual for causing change.

If a poet feels, on the other hand (to quote an easygoing character in one of my own poems), that the human predicament "is just a good bind to be in," the poem should be read as an occasional poem, occasioned by some instance—however flawed or imperfect—of an existing order. An apologist poem aspires to be a celebration.

If a poet thinks of himself only as a man or woman speaking to men and women, the poem should be read simply as poem. A solitary's poem is a message written on one person's clean slate to be copied on another person's clean slate as an exercise in person-hood. A solitary poem wants to become a little universe or a charade.

It is my cheerful illusion that these are fairly clear distinctions to apply to modern poems. Though I apply them to poems, they reflect intentions, brief or long-standing, of the poet who aligns himself with them. They shade into one another, and readers would disagree about many borderline cases. But at best, they could be helpful in determining how a poem wants to be read.

Here is an attractive example of a militant poem, by a poet who I think was twelve years old at the time.

The Cemetery Bridge

Well, as you all should know, there's a dead man
in the George Washington Bridge.
How he got there, they was digging and drilling
these real deep holes for the pillows
of the George Washington Bridge.
While they was digging and drilling, a man fell in.
Of course he was dead, but we will never know for sure.
So they pay his family millions of dollars
so they won't have to dig him up and start all over again.
Please spread this story around.

Terrence Des Pres, a very gifted prose writer, believes that all serious writing today must be politically committed writing, militant writing. In a letter he wrote to me soon after we had debated this for the first time, he put it this way: "Most Anglo-American poetry (excluding old guys like Milton and Blake) looks at life and says, that's how it is, that's the human condition. Political poetry also says that's how things are, but then, instead of settling for the hard comfort of some 'human condition,' it goes on to say, this is not how things must be always. Not even death is that final, when you consider that some men are forced to die like dogs, while others have the luck to die human. Political poetry is concerned with precisely this distinction. And if, by way of example, we ardently oppose the designs of state and the powers that be—as, say, during the Viet Nam war years—is this opposition not a true part of our experience? and if so, is it not a fit subject for poems? Fitter, perhaps than the old laments like lost love, the soul's virginity, etc?"

The poem Terrence Des Pres sent with that letter is by the Polish poet Zbigniew Herbert.

Five Men

1

They take them out in the morning
to the stone courtyard
and put them against the wall
five men
two of them very young
the others middle-aged
nothing more
can be said about them

2

when the platoon
level their guns
everything suddenly appears
in the garish light
of obviousness
the yellow wall
the cold blue
the black wire on the wall

instead of a horizon
that is the moment
when the five senses rebel
they would gladly escape
like rats from a sinking ship
before the bullet reaches its destination
the eye will perceive the flight of the projectile
the ear record a steely rustle
the nostrils will be filled with biting smoke
a petal of blood will brush the palate
the touch will shrink and then slacken
now they lie on the ground
covered up to their eyes with shadow
the platoon walks away
their buttons straps
and steel helmets
are more alive
than those lying beside the wall

3

I did not learn this today
I knew it before yesterday
so why have I been writing
unimportant poems on flowers
what did the five talk of
the night before the execution
of prophetic dreams
of an escapade in a brothel
of automobile parts
of a sea voyage
of how when he had spades
he ought not to have opened
of how vodka is best
after wine you get a headache
of girls
of fruit
of life
thus one can use in poetry
names of Greek shepherds
one can attempt to catch the colour of morning sky
write of love
and also

> once again
> in dead earnest
> offer to the betrayed world
> a rose

The intention of Herbert's subtle and moving poem seems to be to convert poets from writing the old laments like lost love, the soul's virginity, etc., and to enlist them in action to change their political circumstances, if not indeed their own political natures. The poem does not simplify. It retains the demanding reticence of poetry. As a conscience, the reader responds, or not, to its call for change, as clear and ambiguous as Rilke's "You must change your life."

Here is a third example of dissident poetry, a fragment of one of June Jordan's powerful statements about our society's way with black citizens. Irony is its heavy device, but it is pure enough poetry not to say all it means, not to mean only what it says.

Poem: On the Murder of Two Human Being Black Men,
Denver A. Smith and his unidentified Brother,
at Southern University, Baton Rouge, Louisiana, 1972

What you have to realize is about private property
like
for example do you know how much the president's
house weighs in at
do you know that?
But see it's important because obviously
that had to be some heavy building some kinda
heavy heavy bricks and whatnot
dig
the students stood outside the thing
outside of it
and also
on the grass belonging to somebody else (although
who the hell can tell who owns the grass)
but
well the governor/he said the students
in addition
to standing outside the building that was

The House of The President
in addition to that and in addition to
standing on the grass that was growing
beside that heavy real estate
in addition (the governor said) the students
used
quote vile language unquote and
what you have to realize about quote
vile language unquote
is what you have to realize about private property
and
that is
you and your mother and your father and your
sister and your brother
you
and you and you
be strictly lightstuff on them scales
be strictly human life
be lightstuff
weighing in at zero
plus
you better clean your language up
don't be calling mothafuckas *mothafuckas*
pigs *pigs*
animals *animals*
murderers *murderers*
you
weighing less than blades of grass the last
dog peed on
less than bricks smeared grey by pigeon shit
less than euphemisms for a mercenary and
a killer
you be lightstuff
lightstuff on them scales

For all that it is implicit, in these three poems we have just
looked at, that the role of the dissident is the most *urgent* role
at a time like ours, I think there is never any deliberate choos-
ing, except on grounds of temperament—the poem's or the
poet's—between the three roles. The time is always *a time like
ours*. Ours is simply the one we must respond to truly. Each of
the three responses I am trying to delineate asks a great deal

of the writer and the reader. The three short poems I offer as examples of apologist poems don't shirk moral responsibility, but rather contain it within a system whose imperfection they take as given. The imperfections of society, in the poems about equating money with life (in "The Cemetery Bridge"), or countenancing political murders (in "Five Men"), or race murder (in June Jordan's poem) can *only* be responded to militantly, by poet and reader. The imperfections in human nature exhibited in the next three poems are sources of grief but lie beyond grievance. They invite various and complex response.

On Looking for Models
by Alan Dugan

The trees in time
have something else to do
besides their treeing. What is it.
I'm a starving to death
man myself, and thirsty, thirsty
by their fountains but I cannot drink
their mud and sunlight to be whole.
I do not understand these presences
that drink for months
in the dirt, eat light,
and then fast dry in the cold.
They stand it out somehow,
and how, the Botanists will tell me.
It is the "something else" that bothers
me, so I often go back to the forests.

Traveling through the Dark
by William Stafford

Traveling through the dark I found a deer
dead on the edge of the Wilson River road.
It is usually best to roll them into the canyon:
that road is narrow; to swerve might make more dead.

By glow of the tail-light I stumbled back of the car
and stood by the heap, a doe, a recent killing;
she had stiffened already, almost cold.
I dragged her off; she was large in the belly.

My fingers touching her side brought me the reason—
her side was warm; her fawn lay there waiting,
alive, still, never to be born.
Beside that mountain road I hesitated.

The car aimed ahead its lowered parking lights;
under the hood purred the steady engine.
I stood in the glare of the warm exhaust turning red;
around our group I could hear the wilderness listen.

I thought hard for us all—my only swerving—,
then pushed her over the edge into the river.

The Whipping
by Robert Hayden

The old woman across the way
    is whipping the boy again
and shouting to the neighborhood
    her goodness and his wrongs.

Wildly he crashes through elephant ears,
    pleads in dusty zinnias,
while she in spite of crippling fat
    pursues and corners him.

She strikes and strikes the shrilly circling
    boy till the stick breaks
in her hand. His tears are rainy weather
    to woundlike memories:

My head gripped in bony vise
    of knees, the writhing struggle
to wrench free, the blows, the fear
    worse than blows that hateful

Words could bring, the face that I
    no longer knew or loved. . . .
Well, it is over now, it is over,
    and the boy sobs in his room,

And the woman leans muttering against
    a tree, exhausted, purged—
avenged in part for lifelong hidings
    she has had to bear.

My third category will probably strike readers as having the same spinelessness as the category *other* in a quiz or *don't know* in a poll. But in the art which speaks most eloquently for human peculiarity, the poet as solitary seems as serious and deliberate as the socially active or passive poet. He is not at odds with either of them but for the moment removed from them by some concern he can share only person-to-person. Here then are three solitary poems.

The Boxcar Poem
by David Young

The boxcars drift by
clanking

they have their own
speech on scored
wood their own
calligraphy
Soo Line
they say in meadows
Lackawanna quick at crossings
Northern Pacific, a
nightmurmur, Northern
Pacific

even empty
they carry
in dark corners
among smells of wood and sacking
the brown wrappings of sorrow
the rank straws and revolution
the persistence of war

and often
as they roll past
like weathered obedient
angels you can see
right through them
to yourself
in a bright
field, a crow
on either shoulder.

Keeping Things Whole
by Mark Strand

In a field
I am the absence
of field.
This is
always the case.
Wherever I am
I am what is missing.
When I walk
I part the air
and always
the air moves in
to fill the spaces
where my body's been.
We all have reasons
for moving.
I move
to keep things whole.

The Bear
by David Fisher

Thrown from the boxcar of the train, the bear
rolls over and over. He sits up
rubbing his nose. This must be
some mistake,
　　　　there is no audience here.
He shambles off through the woods.
The forest is veined with trails,
he does not know which to follow.
The wind is rising, maple leaves turn up
their silver undersides in agony, there is a
smell in the air, and the lightning strikes.
He climbs a tree to escape. The rain
pours down, the bear is blue as a gall.
　　　　　　　*

There is not much to eat
in the forest, only berries,
and some small delicious animals
that live in a mound and bite your nose.
　　　　　　　*

The bear moves sideways through a broom-straw field.
He sees the hunters from the corner of his eye
and is sure they have come to take him back.
To welcome them, (though there is no calliope)
he does his somersaults, and juggles
a fallen log, and something
    tears through his shoulder,
he shambles away in the forest and cries.
Do they not know who he is?
              *

After a while, he learns to fish, to find
the deep pool and wait for the silver trout.
He learns to keep his paw up for spiderwebs.
There is only one large animal, with trees
on its head, that he cannot scare.
              *

At last he is content to be
alone in the forest,
though sometimes he finds a clearing
and solemnly does his tricks,
though no one sees.

A poem like Zbigniew Herbert's "Five Men" must necessarily imply that its reasons are the most urgent reasons a poem can have, that other reasons are somehow trivial. Poems themselves are sometimes bullies, or seem to be. But this is true only as one hypothesis precludes another. Poetry has always resisted being used as propaganda simply because, like other fully created things, it contains and rejoices in contradictions. "When you organize one of the contradictory elements out of your work of art," Randall Jarrell tells us, "you are getting rid not just of it, but of the contradiction of which it was a part; and it is the contradictions in works of art which make them able to represent to us—as logical and methodical generalizations cannot—our world and our selves." Contradiction, complexity, mystery—these are not useful qualities in propaganda.

If some of my suggestions about how to *open* ourselves as readers are valid, they mean that we must be ready to be astonished, even when that is uncomfortable and morally expensive. When we engage a poem we should credit it with infinite options, not just the three which I have labored, which may strike the reader as obvious or incomplete or wrong. Whatever a poem is up to, it requires our trust along with our consent to let it try to change our way of thinking and feeling. Nothing without this risk. I expect hang gliding must be like poetry. Once you get used to it, you can't imagine not wanting the scare of it. But it's more serious than hang gliding. Poetry is the safest known mode of human risk. You risk only staying alive.

The Reason for Criticism

I see the chief similarity between criticism and poetry as this: they are truest to themselves when their impulse is generous and catholic. If poetry is accurate praise, then criticism should aspire to be accurate praise of praise. The second part of this essay will introduce three of my own poems, in an immodest attempt to show a similarity between the two forms of praise. It will be anecdotal, when it is not downright chatty.

Long before Randall Jarrell had condemned our age, in an essay of that name, as "The Age of Criticism," Robert Frost had said he *never read criticism.* His remark is reminiscent of a story from New Hampshire that dates from the early days of television. There's a little village in northern New Hampshire which I believe still closes its ballot booth early so that it can attract national attention as the first township to record presidential returns. In the first election after we had visible reporters, an NBC correspondent traveled there to walk the morning streets and interview citizens. The well-prepared reporter stopped an old lady and asked her if she would be willing to tell the TV audience how she had voted. He gave her and the viewers a little civics lesson, telling her that he knew the privacy of the ballot was a sacred thing, nowhere more jealously guarded than in New England, etc. The encounter seemed to puzzle the old lady, so that the question, along with the sententious democracy, had to be repeated. Then she said sharply, "Oh, I never vote. It only encourages them."

I'm afraid Frost's refusal to read criticism bespoke the same

Poetry Consultant's Annual Address, delivered at the Library of Congress, May 5, 1980. First published by the Library of Congress, 1982.

exasperated irresponsibility. He once said that his idea of good criticism would be for two intelligent friends to sit together over a good book—it was Milton's *Comus* he gave as an example—and let the first reader point to a couple of lines and then pass the book to the second. This friend would read the passage over until he could, with conviction, nod. Then he would find another line or two that were similarly fraught for him, and pass the book back. Thus what had been said with genius would be partaken among intelligence.

I take the meaning of this dry parable to be: what can be marveled at in a work of art is marvelous *in its own terms,* and that in the manner of Calvinism, either one marvels or one is cast out from marveling. Art resists criticism in the same way it resists paraphrase. Thus Flannery O'Conner wrote, "A story is a way to say something that can't be said any other way. . . . When somebody asks you what a story is about, the only proper thing is to tell him to read the story." The critic, Frost and O'Conner seem to be saying, can only point to a poem or story, or to a crucial passage in the poem or story. But many critics are like boring hosts who describe their self-explanatory travel pictures, standing the while between us and the screen or perhaps even between the projector and the screen. It becomes clear that what they are really pointing at is themselves.

"Criticism *does* exist, doesn't it," Randall Jarrell asks, as if to reassure himself that he is among reasonable people, "for the sake of the plays and stories and poems it criticizes?" And making the same assumption in *The Dyer's Hand,* W. H. Auden goes on to tell how the critic can hope to serve the work he addresses:

> What is the function of a critic? So far as I am concerned, he can do me one or more of the following services:
>
> 1) Introduce me to authors or works of which I was hitherto unaware.
>
> 2) Convince me I have undervalued an author or a work because I had not read them carefully enough.
>
> 3) Show me relations between works of different ages and cultures which I should never have seen for myself because I do not know enough and never shall.

(This third function is abashing. Few of us are comfortable traversing the mythical desert of Wystan Hugh Auden's ignorance.)

4) Give a "reading" of a work which increases my understanding of it.
5) Throw light upon the process of artistic "Making."
6) Throw light upon the relation of art to life, to science, economics, religion, etc.

I have come to love this intimidating definition of criticism because it assumes that the critic and his reader, whatever their inequalities, are both looking at the work as if it were more interesting than themselves. This is the way I believe an artist looks at his work while he is creating it, and the critical insight is bound to profit from approaching the work in the same spirit. One would be embarrassed to say anything so obvious if one were not continually embarrassed by the vanity of criticism.

In the same essay, Auden writes:

If good literary critics are rarer than good poets or novelists, one reason is the nature of human egoism. A poet or a novelist has to learn to be humble in the face of his subject matter which is life in general. But the subject matter of a critic, before which he has to learn to be humble, is made up of authors, that is to say, of human individuals, and this kind of humility is much more difficult to acquire. It is far easier to say—"Life is more important than anything I can say about it" than to say—"Mr. A's work is more important than anything I can say about it."

Attacking bad books is not only a waste of time but also bad for the character. If I find a book really bad, the only interest I can derive from writing about it has to come from myself, from such display of intelligence, wit and malice as I can contrive. One cannot review a bad book without showing off.

The injunction "Resist not evil but overcome evil with good" may in many spheres of life be impossible to obey literally, but in the sphere of art it is common sense. Bad art is always with us, but any given work of art is bad in a period way; the particular kind of badness it exhibits will pass away and be succeeded by some other kind. It is unnecessary, therefore, to attack it, because it will perish anyway. . . . The only sensible procedure for a critic is to keep silent about works which he believes to be bad, while at the same time vigorously campaigning for those he believes to be good, especially if they are being neglected or underestimated by the public. . . .

Some books are undeservedly forgotten; none are undeservedly remembered.

The only time Robert Frost spoke to me about my poems was at a luncheon in the dining room of the Westbury Hotel in New York, where neither of us was at home, between (his) trains. What he said was something like this.

"Your poems are all right, I guess. But you may be getting tired of talking about yourself. It might be a good idea to look at some dramatic poems. There's not enough of that around now. You might want to look at Browning's monologues again, and some of Tennyson's, some of Robinson's. Maybe some of mine. Some things you can say better if you can get someone else to say them for you."

I'd heard him say on another occasion, when someone had mistaken "The Road Not Taken" for a self-portrait, that that poem had been written to tease his shy and indecisive friend Edward Thomas. "Can you imagine *me* saying anything *with a sigh?*"

And once he said, about "Mending Wall," that the neighbor farmer who says "Good fences make good neighbors"—that that character rather than the first person speaker was himself. "When I say me in a poem, it's someone else. When I say somebody else, it might be me."

"Everything written is as good as it is dramatic," he wrote in the introduction to his not very dramatic *A Way Out,* the little one-act play he never allowed to be reprinted.

Soon after our unlikely luncheon—I'm trying to suggest that the Westbury is excessively couth in ways neither of us aspired to—I was working on a poem about atoms. I had been sitting in on a freshman astronomy class, and Robert Bless, the very bright instructor, had said, simply in passing, that it was fortunate for the human animal that we had been fashioned to the scale we were. If we had been only a thousand times larger, we would be able to triangulate, with our wide-spaced eyes, and would have known from the start, by looking at the stars, that we were insignificant to an unnerving degree. On the other hand, if we'd been made a thousand times smaller, we would be able to see one another's pulsing atomic structure, which might have caused interpersonal mistrust even greater than at present.

Well, I was manipulating this data as it affected intelligent, interesting, sensitive, and charming me, and the muse was not warming to our subject. It must have been in an exasperated attempt to use Frost's advice that I gave the poem away. I gave it to a fourteen-year-old high-school student, approximately one-third my then age. I put him in Beloit, Wisconsin, where I'd once spent a night. And I made him black. These three mystifications seem to have enabled me to dramatize a mystery which, in my own character, I was only managing to explain away. This is the poem.

Walter Jenks' Bath

These are my legs. I don't have to tell them, legs,
Move up and down or which leg. They are black.
They are made of atoms like everything else,
Miss Berman says. That's the green ceiling
Which on top is the Robinson's brown floor.
This is Beloit, this is my family's bathroom on the world.
The ceiling is atoms, too, little parts running
Too fast to see. But through them running fast,
Through Audrey Robinson's floor and tub
And the roof and air, if I lived on an atom
Instead of on the world, I would see space.
Through all the little parts, I would see into space.

Outside the air it is all black.
The far apart stars run and shine, no one has to tell them,
Stars, run and shine, or the same who tells my atoms
Run and knock so Walter Jenks, me, will stay hard and real.
And when I stop the atoms go on knocking,

Even if I died the parts would go on spinning,
Alone, like the far stars, not knowing it,
Not knowing they are far apart, or running,
Or minding the black distances between.
This is me knowing, this is what I know.

Robert Frost was generous to me in a number of ways. When the biographical pendulum swings, he will be known for quite a different man than the present vogue for monsters has conjured up. But "Walter Jenks' Bath" was a critical gift from Frost, a poem his critical insight had enabled me to find.

He turned to me once when I was traveling to California with him—turned *on* me, if I wanted to read the body language with which he delivered the question—and asked, in no context whatever, "You're not going to write about me, are you?" I replied defensively, as I do now, "Only to correct error, Robert."

Here's an egregious piece of error—out of the herd, as egregious used to mean—of ungenerous criticism that's been roaming the literary savannahs since Frost died. Before I offer it, let me quote civilized Randall Jarrell again, who incidentally wrote some permanently useful appreciation of Frost. In the first paragraph of what he terms his *complaint* against the age of criticism, he said: "I will try to spare other people's [feelings] by using no names at all." I too refrain from identifying the ill-tempered remarks I'm going to quote. Yet it's interesting how Jarrell manages to call names anonymously, as it were. His language seems to rant *ad hominem* when he levels certain charges:

Item: "A great deal of this criticism . . . is not only bad or mediocre, it is *dull;* it is, often, an astonishingly graceless, joyless, humorless, long-winded, niggling, blinkered, methodical, self-important, cliché-ridden, prestige-obsessed, almost autonomous criticism."

Item: (Speaking of the way critics look down on the literary insights of creative artists) "In the same way, if a pig wandered up to you during a bacon-judging contest, you would say impatiently, 'Go away, pig! What do you know about bacon?' "

Item: "Many critics are bad, I think, because they have spent their life in card-indexes. . . . If works of art were about card-indexes the critic could prepare himself for them in this way, but as it is he cannot."

We need this kind of name-calling, where error is turned into allegorical drama. In quoting the two critical lapses, the two dreadful pieces of slanderous criticism, below, I hope readers will take them as allegories of the character any of us can become when he tries to write of that which he cannot praise.

The criticism is followed immediately by my poem, which intends a kind of appreciation of Frost's life and work. Both address the charge of lying. I maintain that in his life and work Frost understood that telling the truth is the difficult name of both games, life and poetry:

It is not that Frost was cold, that he was a tyrant as well as a coward, that he could no more forgive a generous than a selfish act (the former a judgment, the latter a threat), that he treated his friends as if they were enemies and his enemies as if they were himself. No. The shock is that he was from start to finish, and in nearly every aspect of his life, a successful liar. Exposures which to other men might have been the moral lesson and warning of a lifetime were to Frost merely hints that he ought to refine his tactics. To him, age brought only a new birth of vanity, new interests to protect, a thousand new reasons for hoarding all the old deceptions. This makes him terrifying.

Along with Whitman, Dickinson and Stevens, Frost has a place among the greatest of American writers. We know something about the lives of all these poets and they were all isolated souls. Dickinson was fierce in her detachment, Whitman troubled by it, Stevens at perfect ease. Frost is really in a different class: a more hateful human being cannot have lived who wrote words that moved other human beings to tears. Filled with hate, and worth hating: after reading these three careful volumes, one feels that to stand in the same room with a man about whom one knew a quarter of the things one now knows about Frost would be more than one could bear.

In Memory of Robert Frost

Everyone had to know something, and what they said
About that, the thing they'd learned by curious heart,
They said well.
      That was what he wanted to hear,
Something you had done too exactly for words,
Maybe, but too exactly to lie about either.
Compared to such talk, most conversation
Is inadvertent, low-keyed lying.

If he walked in fear of anything, later on
(Except death, which he died with a healthy fear of)
It was that he would misspeak himself. Even his smile
He administered with some care, accurately.
You could not put words in his mouth
And when you quoted him in his presence
There was no chance that he would not contradict you.

Then there were apparent samenesses he would not
Be deceived by. The presidents of things,
Or teachers, braggarts, poets
Might offer themselves in stereotype
But he would insist on paying attention
Until you at least told him an interesting lie.
(That was perhaps your field of special knowledge?)
The only reason to lie, he said, was for a purpose:
To get something you wanted that bad.

I told him a couple—to amuse him,
To get something I wanted, his attention?
More likely, respite from that blinding attention,
More likely, a friendship
I felt I could only get by stealing.

What little I'd learned about flying
Must have sweated my language lean. *I'd respect you*
For that if for nothing else, he said not smiling
The time I told him, thirty-two night landings
On a carrier, or thirty-two night catapult shots—
Whatever it was, true, something I knew.

    For more than six years I have been writing about Edward
John Trelawny, the friend of Shelley and Byron who met

those two men near to the time of their tragic deaths, and was associated with both of them even in death. He was an outsize and attractively outrageous man, and probably only the fact that I managed to survive, in character, a friendship with Frost emboldens me to keep Trelawny for an imaginary playmate. Before I am done, I want to do a series of poems about him and about his acquaintances there in Italy and Greece in the 1820s. I have come to like and believe him. I believe he tells by and large generous truths about Shelley and Byron, the former of whom he idolized, the latter of whom he saw plain. That this is temporarily an unfashionable position will be made clear by the following quotation from a review of a recent biography of Trelawny:

"Lies, lies, lies!" Edward Trelawny in his later years would shout when anyone else attempted conversation in his presence; and the widespread delusion that anyone really rude must be sincere gained him in his own day a reputation as a daring exposer of other people's pretences and hypocrisies. Most of his earlier biographers have swallowed whole his own unconscionable lies about his life story and his relations with Byron and Shelley. William St. Clair, in his new biography *Trelawny: The Incurable Romancer,* has not been taken in by his subject. He coolly demonstrates that Trelawny never became a picturesque corsair, but spent his whole time at sea as a sullen and unsuccessful midshipmen, never winning promotion in spite of his family influence, even in a period when other men could become commanders at eighteen. He shows that it was Trelawny's inept design of an unseaworthy boat that caused Shelley's death, and that Trelawny's much boasted intimacy with Shelley actually lasted only six months, and with Byron only eighteen months, and that many of his anecdotes about them are demonstrably untrue. He deflates Trelawny's only real-life romantic adventure, in which, by unerringly attaching himself to the most ruffianly and treacherous of the Greek guerrillas, Trelawny condemned himself to an inglorious part in the Greek War of Independence, and ended up with a shot in the back from a man whom he ought to have been shrewd enough to suspect.

The Trelawny who emerges from this biography is rude, dirty, violent, revengeful, boastful, self-absorbed and totally untruthful; a resentful son, an unkind husband, a callous father, an untrustworthy friend, a rebel only because he hated authority, not because he had any genuine ideals or love of repressed humanity. . . .

For historians and biographers, the only useful thing to know about this odious man is that he knew two great poets and was a liar, so that what he says about them is untrustworthy.

It is to Auden that most of us are indebted for the apropos thing C. G. Lichtenberg, otherwise an unread author to me, said. C. G. Lichtenberg said, "A book is a mirror: if an ass peers into it, you can't expect an apostle to look out."

My poem seems to intend another, and I think a more accurate, account of Trelawny.

Trelawny's Dream

The dark illumination of a storm
and water-noise, chuckling along the hull
as the craft runs tight before it.
Sometimes Shelley's laughter wakes me here,
unafraid, as he was the day he dove
into water for the first time, a wooded pool
on the Arno, and lay like a conger eel
on the bottom—"where truth lies," he said—
until I hauled him up.

But oftener the dream insists on all,
insists on retelling all.
                              Ned Williams is the first
to see the peril of the squall. His shout
to lower sail scares the deck-boy wide-eyed
and cuts off Shelley's watery merriment.
The big wind strokes the cat-boat like a kitten.
Riding the slate-grey hillocks, she is dragged
by the jib Ned Williams leaves to keep her head.
The kitten knows the wind is a madman's hand
and the bay a madman's lap.
As she scuds helpless, only the cockney boy
Charles Vivian and I, a dreamer and a child,
see the felucca loom abeam. Her wet lateen
ballooning in the squall, she cuts across

wind and seas in a wild tack, she is on us.
The beaked prow wrenches the little cabin
from the deck, tosses the poet slowly to the air—
he pockets his book, he waves to me and smiles—
then to his opposite element,
light going into darkness, gold into lead.
The felucca veers and passes, a glimpse of a face
sly with horror on her deck. I watch our brave
sailor boy stifle his cry of knowledge
as the boat takes fatal water, then Ned's stricken face,
scanning the basalt waves
for what will never be seen again except in dreams.

All this was a long time ago, I remember.
None of them was drowned except me
whom a commotion of years washes over.
They hail me from the dream, they call an old man
to come aboard, these youths on an azure bay.
The waters may keep the dead, as the earth may,
and fire and air. But dream is my element.
Though I am still a strong swimmer
I can feel this channel widen as I swim.

I have intruded these last two poems because I think they
make the point that even very impressionistic and oblique
praise can enlighten a subject critically more effectively than
the most attentive destructive act. It is interesting that the two
reviewers I have quoted were both talking, in the quotations,
not about the biography purporting to be under review but
instead are reviewing the lives of the dead men.

To be sure, the critic has responsibility to define and identify
excellence, and this implies comparative judgments. These,
too, are useful in proportion as they are generous. Comparison
can be constructive. I will conclude with a paragraph of Jar-
rell's, where he wants to praise Whitman's genius for free
verse, and to compare it with the limiting conventional prosody
of one of Whitman's greatest contemporaries, Tennyson. Note
the respect and affection—which amounts to praise—for Ten-
nyson that emerges from this nice comparison, intended only
for the aggrandizement of Whitman. Jarrell has been quoting
the "Song of Myself":

I understand the large hearts of heroes,
The courage of present times and all times,
How the skipper saw the crowded and rudderless wreck of
   the steam-ship, and Death chasing it up and down
   the storm,
How he knuckled tight and gave not back an inch, and was
   faithful of days and faithful of nights,
And chalked in large letters on a board, Be of good cheer, we
   will not desert you;
How he follow'd with them and tack'd with them three days
   and would not give it up,
How he saved the drifting company at last,
How the lank loose-gown'd women looked when boated from
   the side of their prepared graves,
How the silent old-faced infants and the lifted sick, and the
   sharp-lipp'd unshaved men;
All this I swallow, it tastes good, I like it well, it becomes mine,
I am the man, I suffered, I was there.

In the last lines of this quotation Whitman has reached—as
great writers always reach—a point at which criticism seems
not only unnecessary but absurd: these lines are so good that
even admiration feels like insolence, and one is ashamed of
anything that one can find to say about them. How anyone can
dismiss or accept patronizingly the man who wrote them, I do
not understand.

The enormous and apparent advantages of form, of omis-
sion and selection, of the highest degree of organization, are
accompanied by important disadvantages—and there are far
greater works than *Leaves of Grass* to make us realize this. But if
we compare Whitman with that very beautiful poet Alfred
Tennyson, the most skillful of all Whitman's contemporaries,
we are at once aware how much Tennyson has had to leave out,
even in those discursive poems where he is trying to put every-
thing in. Whitman's poems *represent* his world and himself
much more satisfactorily than Tennyson's do his. In the past a
few poets have both formed and represented, each in the high-
est degree; but in modern times what controlling, organizing,
selecting poet has created a world with as much in it as Whit-
man's, a world that so plainly *is* the world?

The Language of Poetry in Defense
of Human Speech

1. One's native language looks and sounds strange when one begins to read it with the eyes and ears of an international audience, particularly an audience of poets.

2. Instinct tells me that because we are poets we can best exchange our thoughts about this sacred subject, across the chasm of translation, in brief propositions bald enough to be challenged directly. (They must then run the risk of being so bald as to be obvious.)

3. T. S. Eliot wrote: "The poetry of a people takes its life from the people's speech and in turn gives life to it." It would be easier to demonstrate this, however, in Elizabethan England than in the United States today. Very few modern poets are so widely read that their work can be said to give life to modern American speech. (For every phrase contributed to the common idiom by a contemporary poet, like Auden's "the age of anxiety" or Eliot's "not with a bang but a whimper" or Frost's "Good fences make good neighbors" there must be fifty of Shakespeare's phrases we use almost unconsciously— "brave new world," "full of sound and fury," "this petty pace.")

4. When a culture uses its poets hard, their language takes on the muscle tone of athletes, as it did in Elizabethan England. The Elizabethan poets exploited an energy which the

---

These remarks were delivered at the International Poetry Festival at Struga on Lake Ohrid in Yugoslavia, August 24, 1979. They were later reprinted in the *American Poetry Review.*

language developed in the lives of men and women, refined it, and gave it back to them.

5. When poets write for small audiences, their words have the softer musculature of amateur athletes. They contend intramurally, with one another and with good books. Sometimes their language doesn't get enough fresh air or exercise.

6. The best poems written in America this century resonate in the lives of few and presumably atypical American readers. Often these poems obtain great beauty, force, and accuracy of language—I think of Robert Lowell's language as I write this—but they do not nourish the speech of the country except very indirectly: they make the thoughts and feelings of a few men and women more articulate.

7. When these men and women want to say in public the thoughts and feelings which they have apprehended through poems, they must translate the verbal accuracy of the poet into something less exact which the average person understands. This is the cost to language of a culture which does not make general use of its poetry.

8. In our situation the French aphorism is exact; traduire c'est trahire, to translate is to traduce. But where the poet addresses everyone or where everyone addresses himself to poetry, such translation is unnecessary.

9. For years *Poetry* magazine in Chicago used to carry on its back cover a warning from Walt Whitman: "To have great poetry there must be great audiences." In an anti-world somewhere, an anti-Whitman seems to have heard this and decreed what has come to pass in Whitman's land: To have little poets, you must have little audiences.

10. For poetry to become more useful in the United States, it must direct itself to a larger audience, use the language which is most alive among that audience, and provide more accessible delight. (Because people find substitutes for what is denied them.) One of Eliot's characters in "The Waste Land" says:

> He's been in the army four years, he wants a good time.
> And if you don't give it to him there's others will.

(If the poets don't give it to them television will.)

11. When I am writing a poem, in the State of Connecticut, in the United States of America, in 1979, I listen not only to the content of the poem but for words which the people of my time and place would hear as the most precise (and therefore delightful) expression of that content. My listening is deliberately local: a time, a place, a social ambiance. What I hope to hear is a voice, a dialect of the mind.

12. I write a fairly colloquial language, for most purposes, but try to avoid the laziness and slickness which characterize unthinking colloquial speech.

13. The dictionary is there to remind me where words have come from, in our lovely, perverse tongue, and what sort of life they have lived. But it is the writer who keeps the dictionary up to date. His sensibility revises the meanings of words to accommodate new thoughts and feelings which his fellows are trying to think and feel.

14. What the poet is listening for as he writes is the sound a new truth makes. In this sense, his smallest lyric is an act in defense of human speech. He is telling the truth in the language which discovers it. He gives that language to the tribe for further truth-telling uses.

15. Poetry keeps our serious language from hardening into rhetoric. Think of that Victorian New England lady Emily Dickinson shouting to God, when she is bereaved: "Burglar! Banker! Father!" in her exasperation with the decorums of Christian mourning.

16. And poetry reminds us that being honest is not simple. I suppose most languages must have an idiom like "too beautiful (or too anything) for words." The truth is frequently too astonishing for anyone but a poet to word.

17. The language spoken and written in the United States lives by other urgencies than poetry, but it survives. Writers of fine fiction and nonfiction reach a much wider audience than poets, and surely have a strengthening effect on the general precision of language which is constantly being eroded by other forces.

18. Memorable words of politicians, scientists, teachers,

and military and scientific heroes defend human speech, but even a patriotic and optimistic poet does not expect a great volume of memorable words from these sources.

19. Advertisers in the United States attempt the role of poet, coining and redefining words. For the most part, theirs is a contrary intention: to deceive us about the purposes of language. An advertisement seeks to constrain or direct our thoughts and feelings where a poet wants to liberate them. Advertisers (when you include the spoken word on television and radio) manipulate the American language more adversely than all the benign forces combined seem able to keep it true to itself. (Like many American poets, I teach English and have watched this erosion.)

20. The United States is a country with many regions and several cultures. Native Americans, Afro-Americans, and Hispanic Americans were for a long time coerced to assimilate the language we still call English and a culture from Western Europe. Poetry was only one of the values which suffered from this.

21. The millenium has not come, but Americans have lately become more aware of the relationship between language and culture and between culture and human creativity. The States which we are still working to Unite are cultural as well as geographical and political entities. As we have come to recognize this, poetry has emerged in our several languages.

22. To read another dialect of one's own language involves greater possibilities of misunderstanding than to read a language which is manifestly foreign. Readers whose taste and judgment have been trained to "standard English" have not been the most perceptive critics or enjoyers (ideally the same thing) of works in unfamiliar uses of their own language.

23. Even among the recognized practitioners of "standard English," American poets have shown great linguistic variety: Emerson, Whitman, and Dickinson in the nineteenth century are no more alike than Frost, Eliot, and Williams in the twentieth.

24. The American poet typically creates his own role, deciding who he is, what he's for, what language his tribesmen speak, and what he can do for them in it, in character.

25. Contrary to much domestic and foreign opinion, ignorance is not a tradition of American poets, though in their great originality some poets may have given this impression. Saul Bellow spoke for most American writers, I believe, when he defined a writer as a "reader who is moved to emulation."

26. Many American poets today, including some distinguished ones visiting Struga this summer, believe that major new directions for poetry in our country will derive from the aesthetic innovations of European and Latin American poets. This, too, is an American tradition.

27. The dialect of the mind is a very personal speech finally. It hears its own affinities everywhere and tries to speak them truly.

28. Human speech is a great family of such dialects. Only if each language is capable of the accuracy of poetry can we hope to exchange the ideas we value most, those shy and complex needs we call brotherhood and love.

" 'Do Not Embrace Your Mind's New Negro Friend' "

Lately I have been reading through the four books of verse—perhaps 130 poems, mostly lyrics—that represent my entire title to the name of poet. I have decided the reason they are so few is not primarily laziness (although I agree with what I think was Robert Frost's opinion that laziness, *of a certain kind,* is a grace attractive to the Muse, just as busyness, of a certain kind, strikes her as vulgar). Chiefly I think my poverty of output stems from the conviction that an unnecessary poem is an offence to the art. What I would like to do in these remarks is clarify a little for myself and the reader what I mean by *unnecessary.*

The poem I am using as an example of the necessary is probably a rather disposable item of the 1940s. That is to say its integrity, as poem, may be provincial. But it *is,* or maybe only *was,* a necessary poem for me. Its subject—Civil Rights, I guess we would call it today—is a concern that my generation grew up with and have, on the whole, showed some responsibility about. But when this poem was written I was about twenty-eight and my feeling about Negroes and Jews and other minorities was that of a young man much of whose adult life had been spent in military service and little of whose life had been spent familiarly with any except White Anglo-Saxon Protestants. At this point I should introduce the poem:

In *Corgi Modern Poets in Focus: 2,* edited by Jeremy Robson (Corgi Books, 1971).

"Do Not Embrace Your Mind's New Negro Friend"

Do not embrace your mind's new Negro friend
Or embarrass the blackballed Jew with memberships:
There must be years of atonement first, and even then
You may still be the blundering raconteur
With the wrong story, and they may still be free.

If you are with them, if even mind is friend,
There will be plenty to do: give the liars lessons
Who have heard no rumors of truth for a long time
But have whatever they hear on good authority,
Whether it concerns Chinese women or the arts.

Expose the patrons, some of whose best friends
Are brothers, and who are never now anonymous:
What kind of credit do they expect for that,
Ask them, or better, ask their protested brothers,
The grateful tenants who can't get their curtsies right.

Finally the injured, who think they have no friend,
Who have been convinced by the repeated names
That they are Jews or Negroes or some dark thing:
They must be courted with the lover's touch
And as guiltily as if yourself had turned them inward.

If you complete this program, you will have friends
From all the rich races of your human blood:
Meantime, engage in the often friendless struggle.
A long war, a pygmy war in ways,
But island by island we must go across.

The poem suggests the beginning in me of a responsibility (I don't like to call it a guilt, because that word is so often used to suggest gloomy irresponsibility) about the most interesting and hopeful event of modern America. In the same volume with it, and I was almost twenty-nine when it went to press, are some marvellously callow accounts of a less interesting America. But this poem seems to me *necessary* in the following terms. In it an aspiring poet, me, confronted something he did not understand: the inability of his culture to treat people with the respect and affection to which they were individually entitled. The Civil Rights movement has come a long way, and I blush a little at the innocence of the poem. But coming across it in the literature of the forties I would not feel it was naïve historically. It is in fact a poem, feeling out a problem warily and with the powers of attention the poet could muster.

The files of the *Nation* for 1947 would be more interesting historically. In the same sense, the files of the *New York Times* during the Depression are more interesting historically than Robert Frost's beautiful poem about bureaucracy called "Departmental." Poems have to be more sophisticated than history. Frost was not a politician, and I am not, even now, after three scary summers of teaching Negro high-school kids, a Negro Leader. But when I wrote that poem, I had the kind of impulse that I feel the Muse approves. I was exploring, mostly for myself, a puzzle about which I had a glimmering. Maybe that is the likeliest prescription for a work of art: a puzzle about which one has a glimmering.

Now the difference between a poet's approach to his glimmering and that of a practical man is like the difference between art and propaganda. Art makes the error, in practical terms, of recognizing alternatives. It's a curious thing how certain angry works, works conceived in anger, like Goya's *Disasters of War* or *Madame Bovary,* are without propaganda value: *after such knowledge, what forgiveness?* they seem to say.

(My aunt, who comes from Alabama, is reported to have said on seeing the title of the poem, "Well, I should hope not!" It is hard to read the poems of one's relatives as poems, but she was taking the matter too personally.)

The fact that it *is* a poem, of whatever quality, seems to the middle-aged man commenting on it now, demonstrable in a couple of ways. One is that the diction, by and large, is natural—something that cannot be said for half the poems in the volume with it. Another is that its form seems to grow fairly naturally out of its self-discovery. I have recently been teaching John Berryman's poem "Winter Landscape," which seems to have fallen into five stanzas of five-foot verse with an elegance beyond my present skill, although Berryman wrote it at perhaps half my age. Nevertheless, my poem seems to me to have felt out a certain cinquefoil rhythm, and allowed that rhythm its trespasses. Like Richard Wilbur, whom I greatly admire, I have been accused of a sterile formality, and unlike

Richard Wilbur, I have sometimes been guilty of it. This poem, and two or three poems a year ever since I was twenty-one, suggest to me that when I pay attention, I find the form of the poem in the course of finding its content. The glimmering that an artist has is incarnate, if it is real. Form and content discover themselves simultaneously.

The Luck of It

A poet approaches language in the spirit of a woodman who asks pardon of the dryad in a tree before he cuts it down. Words are inhabited by the accumulated experience of the tribe. The average poet adds about as much to the language as he adds to the nitrogen content of his native soil. But he can administer the force that resides in words.

It is the magic inhabiting the language that he administers, all the lived meaning that the noises have picked up in the days and nights since they were first uttered. He finds ways to revive that total meaning, or a part of it he wants to use, as he makes his verbal artifacts. His very attentive use of a word, associating it with other words used with equal attention (for no word is an island), astonishes us the way we would be astonished to hear a dryad speak pardon out of an oak tree. And as if this were not all elfin enough already, he does the job largely at a subconscious level. His intelligence stands around, half the time, like a big, friendly, stupid apprentice, handing him lopping-shears when he wants the chain saw.

In "Duns Scotus's Oxford," Hopkins demonstrates this magic of association in the tremendous energy of the opening and closing lines. "Towery city and branchy between towers;"— who would have imagined there was all that going on in those six words before they were joined in that sequence? And of Duns Scotus himself, the final line says, "Who fired France for Mary without spot." *Kinesis* is all, and the energy is in the words rather than in the thinky parts of man's mind.

In *American Poets in 1976,* edited by William Heyen (Bobbs-Merrill, 1976).

Both superstition and modesty warn a poet against reducing his meager knowledge of these forces to theory. A poem I wrote a long time ago has come to seem to me an example of how much luck goes into the job. It was a breakthrough that I seemed at the time simply to stumble on as I went about my fairly methodical and fairly *safe* wording of experience. It was a poem that carried me into its own experience, demonstrating that simple mystery Frost has put: no surprise in the writer, no surprise in the reader. It's a poem called "A View of the Brooklyn Bridge," and I am still incapable of judging it as a poem, so strongly did it imprint itself as a revelation. Set down rationally, revelations sound like hallucination: this bush by the side of the road flared up and a voice spoke out of it—we very rational people feel foolish recounting it. But this is what happened: a series of associations, and the words they inhabited, came to me uninvited but because I was in a state of un-self-centered attention. This is apparently a rare state with me, because in the twenty-five years since then I have averaged about six poems a year. That is apparently as often as the muse can get my attention.

Before I introduce the document, I might say that it had perhaps one forerunner, a longer poem called "Love Letter from an Impossible Land"—a somewhat more willful performance but similar—that I'd written five years earlier, when I was twenty-three. Other than that, I think all the poems I had written before this were primarily rational attempts to word accurately something I thought I understood. This poem, and to a less conscious degree "Love Letter," were irrational acts of surrender to an experience I knew very little about but which I had a sudden sense was being offered to me.

A View of the Brooklyn Bridge

The growing need to be moving around it to see it,
To prevent its freezing, as with sculpture and metaphor,
Finds now skeins, now strokes of the sun in a dark
Crucifixion etching, until you end by caring
What the man's name was who made it,
The way old people care about names and are
Forever seeing resemblances to people now dead.

Of stone and two metals drawn out so
That at every time of day
They speak out of strong resemblances, as:
Wings whirring so that you see only where
Their strokes finish, or: spokes of dissynchronous wheels.

Its pictures and poems could accurately be signed
With the engineer's name, whatever he meant.
These might be called: *Tines inflicting a river, justly,*
Or (thinking how its cables owe each something
To the horizontal and something to the vertical):
A graph of the odds against
Any one man's producing a masterpiece.

Yet far from his, the engineer's, at sunrise
And again at sunset when,
Like the likenesses the old see,
Loveliness besets it as haphazard as genes:
Fortunate accidents take the form of cities
At either end; the cities give their poor edges
To the river, the buildings there
The fair color that things have to be.
Oh the paper reeds by a brook
Or the lakes that lie on bayous like a leopard
Are not at more seeming random, or more certain
In their sheen how to stand, than these towns are.

And of the rivering vessels so and so
Where the shadow of the bridge rakes them once,
The best you can think is that, come there,
A pilot will know what he's done
When his ship is fingered

Like that Greek boy whose name I now forget
Whose youth was one long study to cut stone;
One day his mallet slipped, some goddess willing
Who only meant to take his afternoon,
So that the marble opened on a girl
Seated at music and wonderfully fleshed
And sinewed under linen, riffling a harp;
At which he knew not that delight alone
The impatient muse intended, but, coupled with it, grief—
The harp-strings in particular were so light—
And put his chisel down for marvelling on that stone.

It *is* a poem of associations, isn't it? a gatherer as Robert Frost used to call them. Let me gloss it a little.

I was living near the bridge that winter, and looked at it a lot. In the house where I lived there were two artists who were good talkers and my closest friend was an artist who was a good listener, so I was probably seeing things with freshly peeled eyes. I can't remember where the image of skeins came from—I had to look the word up as I wrote this, but the crucifixion etching was a Rembrandt, I think one I'd seen at the Metropolitan where the wife of one of the painters had a job. I had been more irritated than wondering at my southern grandmother and a French woman I knew who *cared about names and were forever seeing resemblances to people now dead.* But in the openness of the poem I find no irritation (although I suppose the word *forever* is gently irritable), rather an affection for the old, for the associative-recollective process that is characteristic of age and of this poem. It seems to have been a kind of grace I was experiencing—an arrogant person in my late twenties—as I followed whither the poem led.

The image of *spokes of dissynchronous wheels* came into my head from aviation. I was still flying occasionally as a reserve pilot in the Navy, and when you fly propeller planes in formation you adjust the speed of your engine (by adjusting the pitch of your propeller) by looking through the blades of your own propeller at that of the lead plane until the blades appear to be standing still. I wonder what that image conveys, if anything, to a reader who hasn't observed the spokes of dissynchronous wheels or propellers.

When the poem first appeared in a book, I glossed the line about the engineer's name, as follows: "The Brooklyn Bridge was designed by J. A. Roebling who began the work in 1869 which his son W. A. Roebling completed in 1883"—an impulse of propitiation, perhaps? as if the engineer might be helping me with my job?

With one of the three painters in particular, the now well-known Canadian Jack Shadbolt, I used to have very rangy talk. *The odds against any one man's producing a masterpiece* had been the theme of last night's talk.

The paper reeds by a brook is borrowed I think from *Psalms,* but I know it came to me from a beautiful setting by Randall Thompson, a colleague at Princeton the year before. *The lakes that lie on bayous like a leopard*—am I boring you, reader, with all these fingernail clippings?—I had ferried a plane to the west coast that winter by way of Louisiana.

I made up the Greek sculptor and his anecdote, but *made up* is too willful a verb: the Greek boy and his muse came to me, and the story—his wanting to do something difficult with his mallet, and having it done instead without his effort or even consent—came to me as a story that I did not then understand, a story parallel to something that was happening to me in the fashioning, if I did fashion it, of the poem.

A final gloss, comprehensive of the whole forty-seven lines: the things I hadn't read! Whitman, Hart Crane, none of the poem's ancestors.

The opening up of form that occurred in the poem is something that had happened with me before, but more often from clumsiness or laziness than at the direction of the poem. To this day I feel surer that I'm communicating with the poem if a prosodic pattern declares itself. I have sacred texts about this.

> Most of my poetry is metrical, though I have written some free verse, syllabics, etc. One reason I write metrically is very simple: I do this better than I do in the more open forms. But I think I have a more deliberate choice behind it: from first to last most of my poems have dealt with violent or extreme or *non-verbal* [italics mine] experience. Fitting such experience through a fairly fixed form helps me to more firmly re-create it, and so to come to terms with it, possibly even to partially understand it. The openness of the experience is brought into relation with the structures of the mind. (Thom Gunn, in a letter, 1970)

This is a fragment from a dialogue between Borges and a writing student at Columbia University (from *Borges on Writing*, edited by Norman Thomas di Giovanni, Daniel Halpern, and Frank MacShane):

Question: One can read the poets of the past and interpret what is learned into free verse.

Borges: What I fail to understand is why you should *begin* by attempting something that is so difficult, such as free verse.

Question: But I don't find it difficult.

Borges: Well, I don't know your writing, so I can't really say. It might be that it is easy to write and difficult to read.

Auden ("He thanks God daily / that he was born and bred / a British Pharisee," he says of himself elsewhere) talks about the problem as if the devices of prosody were our servants:

> The poet who writes "free" verse is like Robinson Crusoe on his desert island: he must do all his cooking, laundry and darning for himself. In a few exceptional cases, this manly independence produces something original and impressive, but more often the result is squalor—dirty sheets on the unmade bed and empty bottles on the unswept floor. (*The Dyer's Hand*)

But the fourth of these texts is the one I need most, and states the other half of what has to be a dialectic. Randall Jarrell, in his extraordinary appreciation called "Some Lines from Whitman," says:

> The enormous and apparent advantages of form, of omission and selection, of the highest degree of organization, are accompanied by important disadvantages. . . . If we compare Whitman with that very beautiful poet Alfred Tennyson, the most skillful of all Whitman's contemporaries, we are at once aware of how limiting Tennyson's forms have been, of how much Tennyson has had to leave out. . . . Whitman's poems *represent* his world and himself much more satisfactorily than Tennyson's do his. In the past a few poets have both formed and represented, each in the highest degree; but in modern times what controlling, organizing, selecting poet has created a world with as much in it as Whitman's, a world that so plainly *is* the world? (*Poetry and the Age*)

And in the luck of the poem there is one other element: will the poem work as well for the reader as it works for the muse and her scribe? Can you step back from the poem and see what is *there,* having been present when all its bright ambience burned and taken down what the unearthly voice said?

In the magazine where some of my favorite poems have appeared, for more than twenty years, a poem that I thought well enough of to place at the front of my selected poems was read this way:

> William Meredith's volume is prefaced by an elegantly thoughtful foreword in which he tells us that although he may not have kept the most promising poems, he has kept the ones "that try to say things I am still trying to find ways to say, poems that engage mysteries I still pluck at the hems of. . . ." As the patriotic sailor was heard to say, staring out at the mid-Atlantic, it makes you feel kinda humble and kinda proud. Meredith's poetry has all the virtues: decency, reverence, gravity, quiet curiosity, and there is something very depressing about it, as of poetry soft at the center.

The reviewer then quoted only the middle stanza of the opening poem.

Winter Verse for His Sister

Moonlight washes the west side of the house
As clean as bone, it carpets like a lawn
The stubbled field tilting eastward
Where there is no sign yet of dawn.
The moon is an angel with a bright light sent
To surprise me once before I die
With the real aspect of things.
It holds the light steady and makes no comment.

Practicing for death I have lately gone
To that other house
Where our parents did most of their dying,
Embracing and not embracing their conditions.
Our father built bookcases and little by little stopped reading,
Our mother cooked proud meals for common mouths.
Kindly, they raised two children. We raked their leaves
And cut their grass, we ate and drank with them.
Reconciliation was our long work, not all of it joyful.

Now outside my own house at a cold hour
I watch the noncommittal angel lower
The steady lantern that's worn these clapboards thin
In a wash of moonlight, while men slept within,
Accepting and not accepting their conditions,
And the fingers of trees plied a deep carpet of decay
On the gravel web underneath the field,
And the field tilting always toward day.

His comment went on, and I have to confess that I think it's witty, though to this day I have been unable to find a revision of the poem—without betraying what I feel is its discovered language—that will make the metaphors of that second stanza less vulnerable to misfeeling:

What kind of a meal are you cooking? Oh, I think a proud meal tonight. How do you raise your children? Kindly, thank you. It's all too beautiful and shaming to be true, establishing the poet as such a splendid understander, knower and forgiver that a slightly self-congratulatory atmosphere hangs over this poem and the whole volume.

In general, a poet tries to make misreading and mistaking of feeling impossible, by the same attention that he pays to exact rendering of the experience he is being initiated into. Clearly he is not always lucky in both phases of his intuitive work, and there is always somebody waiting at the third stage who can say with critical detachment, Meredith is no Whitman or Tennyson. But what an ordinary poet congratulates himself on is, I suppose, being a good scribe, taking the things down as the tongue declares them. And, of course, the luck of being chosen by the tongue in the first place.

III

On Poets

The Proving Ground

Robert Frost's book of poems makes one wish the dust jacket gang had left unemasculated some single phrase to characterize the event. But, as it is, no one interested in poetry is likely to miss the book, or, reading it, to fail to be taken again by the wisdom and cunning of a great poet and craftsman.

The same sort of uniformity which marked the six earlier collections—one should perhaps call it integrity, to describe a singleness of artistic purpose like Frost's—allows this book to be fitted seamlessly to the last page of *A Further Range.* Indeed Frost's work is all of a piece. Those who had thought to see trends between volume and volume were confounded by the first collected edition, where new poems were inserted in the earliest volume and there was almost no chronology apparent. Only such a poet could have published this last volume, including a poem written last summer and one dated "C1900," without any discrepancy in tone.

A Witness Tree is a slim book, like the others in that respect as in the respect that the poet's personality dominates every poem. The opening sonnet, "The Silken Tent," is a notable demonstration of what Frost has consistently taken to be the chief function of poetry: to explore and set limits to metaphor. This poem, together with "I Could Give All to Time," is surely among the most distinguished of all his lyrics.

The familiar playfulness is present, too; the tight puns, the dry latinisms, the two and three line poems with pretentious titles. And in at least two of the dramatic poems, a strange rustic one called "The Subverted Flower," and a balladlike

New Republic, June 1, 1942.

story called "The Discovery of the Madeiras," there is the same controlled terror that makes scenes from *North of Boston* remain memorable as drama long after the lines are gone.

One would like to report certain of Frost's trademarks missing from this book; readers who had a hard time swallowing those argumentative lines entitled "Build Soil" in the last book will fare hardly better with a couple of long ones in this volume: "The Lesson for Today" and "The Literate Farmer and the Planet Venus," or with a few short poems in which public utilities and GOP come off rather better than Liberal journals of opinion. Mr. Frost has somewhere said that he preferred griefs to grievances in poetry, and the phrase is not one that should be allowed to die.

When another of Robert Frost's books of poems, *North of Boston,* appeared in the last war, there must have been many readers who felt, as they read that "book of people" with its tight New England riddles and sly answers, that it was not a timely book. But that is a sort of timeliness that Frost does not pretend to; he has said before and he says again here that he is concerned with the world primarily as a proving ground for the human soul, a focus which does not make for excitability at the latest turns of history. What he has to say about the human soul, however, is timely enough to last for fine poetry and for many years.

Robert Frost in Book Reviews and under the Aspect of Eternity

The proof of a poet is that his country absorbs him as affectionately as he has absorbed it.

—Walt Whitman

In the Clearing is the latest addition to the most successful work in the progress of poetry in our language. To describe the book this way is only to insist that, in the constancy of its concerns and of its success, Robert Frost's work is a single work. It has grown like a tree of a new species; the layer of live wood is a perennial miracle of new life, but the tree itself is what is altogether astonishing, a new tree even before it was the giant it stands today.

In the almost fifty years that Robert Frost has been publishing books of poetry, twelve reviews have appeared in this magazine, which had started the year before *A Boy's Will.* Perhaps the best were the second one by Ezra Pound (who had also written the first) and the latest one by William Carlos Williams. Most of them were written by poets and they represent articulately the judgments that were made of the work, volume by volume, as it grew, a work that has survived many parochialisms of time and looks as though it would survive them all.

> Things must expect to come in front of us
> A many times—I don't say just how many—
> That varies with the things—before we see them.

Poetry 100, no. 3 (December, 1963). Copyright © 1963 by The Modern Poetry Association. Reprinted by permission of the Editor of *Poetry.*

Brother Meserve tells us in "Snow" and surely this is truer of works of art than of most things.

In 1929 Harriet Monroe, the remarkable woman who fashioned *Poetry*, noticed that the quality of Frost's work was beginning to fall off. This simple, relatively lovable error has been repeated with every book since then, though not often in these pages where it stands as just another of Miss Monroe's famous firsts. The volume she was reviewing contained "Spring Pools," "Once by the Pacific," "Tree at my Window," "The Flood," and "Acquainted with the Night," and it was called *West-Running Brook*. Well, these poems are Frost's all right, that wonderful woman wrote, "but none of them may be ranked among Frost's best. . . . The title poem is a slight affair . . ." etc. (The people who have believed that they invented Robert Frost, and like the telephone and the airplane he is widely claimed, have been particularly subject to this error about new works, which are bound to seem apocryphal if not indeed by a spurious hand.)

Another critical error (which was seen at its most intelligent and pigheaded in George W. Nitchie's book called *Robert Frost: A Study of a Poet's Convictions*) is to review the opinions or philosophy that can be attributed to a poet on the basis of a work or a fragment of a work. But a poet speaks through many characters. He has many visions of the things that deeply concern him. The subjects to which he returns, as Richard Wilbur has observed, are those which vex him. Poems talk to each other about the ambiguities of life. "And there is always more than should be said," Frost himself says in "The Wind and the Rain."

At the end of a rather friendly review of *A Masque of Reason* in 1945 E.S. Forgotson took exception to the poet's view of the responsibility for human trouble. "It had to seem unmeaning to have meaning," Frost's God has said to Job about his suffering. Like the Book of Job, Frost's book is sophisticated enough to lay most of the blame on God.

Mr. Forgotson goes on to say that happily there is a "less stultifying" view of man's plight than this, and then he quotes (you hardly know where to put the *sic!* in a sentence like this) an article by Ruth Benedict from *Partisan Review* to the effect that "the chief evils of our time, such as war and fascism, economic depression and individual neurosis . . . are consequences of man's having arranged his affairs to his own disadvantage." I have no quarrel with this as anthropology, but I can't feel that the "Masque" has been confronted, any more than Mr. Nitchie confronts the poems when he says they yield not gyres nor yew trees and therefore are less serious than Yeats or Eliot.

William Carlos Williams, writing of the second masque in 1948, shows how a poet takes meaning. "There is one thing I will not do in reviewing this book, that is to try to separate the characters from their 'meaning' in order to make that clear for the general reader. That meaning if I judge rightly, was never meant by Mr. Frost to be made clear in that way, rather it was densely integrated with the character and as far as I am concerned must remain so." Since Frost is committed to the view that "everything is as good as it is dramatic," Dr. Williams's position is soundly applicable to the lyric as well as the overtly dramatic poems. Yet most of the people who have quarreled with Frost's stature have done so on the basis of this simple error: they take certain dramatic utterances, few or many, and make a creed of them which they then find insufficient.

As the poems accumulate they give a rather complete account of the universe. It is a compendious rather than an edited account—"at least I will not have it systematic," as one of the independent-minded quatrains says.

The poems in the new book argue with the *Complete Poems* like old cronies. "Pod of the Milkweed" is one of a series of discussions of prodigality, including "November," "Carpe Diem," and "In Hardwood Groves." "Away" takes up the theme of death in a tone like and yet unlike the tones of "Misgiving," "In a Disused Graveyard," "To Earthward," and a dozen others. "A Cabin in the Clearing" reminds you, in its account of the limits of human knowledge, of "Neither Out Far Nor In Deep" and "The Star-Splitter," but in its affection for the householders it reminds you of the young people in poems like "Two Look at Two" and "A Rogers Group." "The Draft Horse" is one of the most perfect poems in the new collection. It reaches back in our minds for all that has been said since *A Boy's Will* about the debate between good and evil.

The Draft Horse

With a lantern that wouldn't burn
In too frail a buggy we drove
Behind too heavy a horse
Through a pitch-dark limitless grove.

And a man came out of the trees
And took our horse by his head
And reaching back to his ribs
Deliberately stabbed him dead.

The ponderous beast went down
With a crack of a broken shaft.
And the night drew through the trees
In one long invidious draft

The most unquestioning pair
That ever accepted fate
And the least disposed to ascribe
Any more than we had to to hate,

We assumed that the man himself
Or someone he had to obey
Wanted us to get down
And walk the rest of the way.

A reviewer who confines himself to pointing to a poem like this, or to the frontispiece poem abstracted from "Kitty Hawk," and saying, this is what I mean by a poem firmly lodged—there is a reviewer playing it safe with posterity.

Selected Letters of Robert Frost

I have written to keep the curious out of the secret places of my mind.

　　　　　　　　　—from a Frost letter to Sidney Cox

I have kept hidden in the instep arch
Of an old cedar at the waterside
A broken drinking goblet like the Grail
Under a spell so the wrong ones can't find it,
So can't get saved, as Saint Mark says they mustn't.

　　　　　　　　　　　　　　　　　　("Directive")

Frost has always given the Wrong Ones a hard time, and this book will only help them damn themselves deeper. He disliked the word compassion, which seemed to stain both giver and taker with crocodile tears, and he liked the word magnanimity, which assumes infinite spirit in the giver and leaves the taker free to put his own price on himself. The wrong ones, as far as his letters and poems are concerned, are those who will not see what he's up to, having their own preconceptions about what he ought to be up to. The letters are like the poems in this: as straightforward as they seem, one by one, they add up to a Masonic mystification. Like the poems, they will mean a lot to the initiate.

They are based on a single secret, which is Frost's identity. He discovered it early, wrestled with it for a lifetime, lived mercilessly to bring it off. It is not a twentieth-century identity and we are not easy with it. What these letters show is how early and with what certainty Frost knew that he was to exist on the scale of Emerson and Browning and Hardy. He ac-

American Scholar 34, no. 1 (Spring 1964).

cepted this bigness and took it to mean he was not to traffic with poets or poetry smaller than himself. He remained in doubt—as probably he had to if he was to go on risking big poems into his eighties—as to how successful he had been. But he seldom doubted the *scale* on which he would succeed or fail. He disguised his identity by humility and vanity—more humility at first, more vanity toward the end—but it seems clear from the letters that there was never an intimacy between Frost and anyone who didn't sense how grandiose was his claim that "the work is play for mortal stakes."

Of the themes that run through the letters none is more insistent than his sense of himself. At the age of twelve he wrote (and this mustn't of course be taken too seriously, but isn't it just the old Frost?): "There are not many girls I like but when I like them I fall dead in love with them and there are not many I like just because I can have some fun with them like I can Lida but I like you because I can't help myself and when I get mad at you I feel mad at myself to." At twenty he writes to the editor who had bought "My Butterfly": "that poem exaggerates my ability. . . . Do not think this artifice or excess of modesty, though, for to betray myself utterly, such an one am I that even in my failures I find all the promise I require to justify the astonishing magnitude of my ambition," and: "I am learning how to spell. I am learning to write better poetry. It is only a matter of time now when I shall throw off the mask and declare for literateur mean it poverty or riches."

Declare for literateur he never did, in the sense that other poets of his time and soon after did. Is it wrong to say of Pound, Eliot, Stevens—everyone else in fact except Yeats—that they played for smaller stakes than Frost, to the extent that they played in the terms of a literary world? Instinctively he kept apart from writers of anywhere near his own stature, and if pride was a motive it seems to have worked in conjunction with other, sounder instincts.

The know-nothing pose was the one that threw most Wrong Ones off-balance. Seen in the letters and in the light of Frost's ambition, this was simply a way of getting shut of a particular provincialism: the provincialism of people who withdraw from a vulgar world into intellectual or artistic concerns. "The beauty of such things as Into My Own, My November Guest, A Dream Pang, Mowing and Reluctance," he wrote in 1913 after *A Boy's Will* came out, "is that they are not just postgraduate work . . . *but the unforced expression of a life I was forced to live.*"

Throughout the letters of this period Frost is feeling out his particular genius as a poet and getting it right. The theory behind his work is strikingly set forth in the several prefaces to his own and other people's work that he published in later years, but it is perfectly consistent with these early letters. At thirty-nine he had written to John Bartlett, a former student: "I alone of English writers have consciously set myself to make music out of what I may call the sound of sense. . . . An ear and an appetite for these sounds of sense is the first qualification of a writer, be it of prose or verse. But if one is to be a poet he must learn to get cadences by skillfully breaking the sounds of sense with all their irregularity of accent across the regular beat of the metre." He had been doing it, too.

As a man, biographical and autobiographical, Frost is like Joyce or Yeats: one either likes or dislikes him strongly, but this judgment can be easily dissociated from the work, which is of course the real and enduring personality. I can't help feeling that the Wrong Ones are missing a lot, but the poems are a good deal more magnanimous than the man ever was to his enemies.

Auden as Critic

And almost thence my nature is subdued
To what it works in, like the dyer's hand:
                                   —Sonnet CXI

I think I am the third poet the editor of this magazine has tried to get to review *The Dyer's Hand,* a major poet's assay of literary criticism, and it has taken me a year and a half to muster the bad judgment to try it. The gates of the book are defended by gargoyles of the superfluous critic. It is a work intended to reprove unnecessary criticism, and it does this both explicitly and by the performance of feats of insight and sensibility that I have come to feel (and the book has been around for almost three years now) are in fact necessary to modern thinking and feeling.

In the early pages, Auden lists six services, one or more of which a critic can perform for him. I would like in this review to claim the two first, and humblest, of these, even though he has apparently disqualified me with the remark that "the first three of these services demand scholarship." These are: "1) To introduce me to authors of works of which I was hitherto unaware." (How many people do you still meet who have not been introduced to *The Dyer's Hand?*) and "2) To convince me that I have undervalued an author or work because I have not read them carefully enough." (And how many are deceived by wit and personality into thinking they have read a work less than serious?) The other four functions that Auden assigns to the critic are more exacting, yet in the course of the book he

Poetry 107, no. 2 (November, 1965). Copyright © 1965 by The Modern Poetry Association. Reprinted by permission of the Editor of *Poetry.*

fulfills them more than once and for a wide variety of works of art.

The service that really belongs to the scholar, "3) To show me relations between works of different ages and cultures which I could never have seen for myself because I do not know enough and never shall"—this he performs very unobtrusively, almost on the sly, as I suppose good scholarship is often performed today. George Peele is set beside Robert Frost, Peer Gynt is contrasted with Falstaff, and everywhere the stories of one time suggest stories of another: it is not your reading that is being broadened but your repertory of tales.

"4) To give a 'reading' of a work which increases my understanding of it." The reading of Falstaff in "The Prince's Dog" may be the most perceptive comment on the character since Verdi, but to quote from it (and this is one of the booby traps lurking everywhere for reviewers of *The Dyer's Hand*) would be to give the misleading impression that the essay is a chain of aphorisms. The essay on D. H. Lawrence's poems is another such reading, and perhaps more susceptible of quotation. After presenting the short autobiographical poem that describes the two worlds of his mother and father, the poem ending "Indoors we called each other you / outside it was tha and thee," Auden writes:

> In formal poetry, the role played by language itself is so great that it demands of the poet that he be as intimate with it as with his own flesh and blood and love it with a single-minded passion. A child who has associated standard English with Mother and dialect with Father has ambivalent feelings about both which can hardly fail to cause trouble for him in later life if he should try to write formal poetry.

The argument about Lawrence's prosody contains these further observations:

> The difference between formal and free verse may be likened to the difference between carving and modeling; the formal poet, that is to say, thinks of the poem he is writing as something already latent in the language which he has to reveal,

while the free verse poet thinks of language as a plastic, passive medium upon which he imposes his artistic conception.

The poems in *Birds, Beast, and Flowers* are among Lawrence's longest. He was not a concise writer and he needs room to make his effect. In his poetry he manages to make a virtue out of what in his prose is often a vice, a tendency to verbal repetition. The recurrence of identical or slightly varied phrases helps to give his free verse a structure; the phrases themselves are not particularly striking, but this is as it should be, for their function is to act as stitches.

The fifth service a critic may perform is to "Throw light upon the process of artistic 'Making.' " This is most clearly undertaken in the opening section of the book where the famous Oxford inaugural lecture 'Making, Knowing, and Judging' appears with two other pieces directly addressing themselves to writing and the writing of poetry. But it is thematic throughout the book, and *The Dyer's Hand* is more than a revelation of Auden's tastes and interests. It is dogmatic with the dogma of a craftsman, and what he says about Lawrence's criticism applies to his own:

> Very few statements which poets make about poetry, even when they appear to be quite lucid, are understandable except in their polemic context. To understand them, we need to know what they are directed against, what the poet who made them considered the principal enemies of genuine poetry.

The polemic context of this book is the maturity of a major poet.

The last and highest opportunity a critic has to serve, Auden says, is to "Throw light upon the relation of art to life, to science, economics, ethics, religion, etc." The book does this, I feel, in the way only a complete and unique human personality can do. A personality—artist or not—is a connective fabric of human experience. Those whose criticism interests us are those whose connections are wide and deep. In speaking of our period, Auden says: "The characteristic style of 'Modern' poetry is an intimate tone of voice, the speech of one person addressing one person, not a large audience; whenever a modern poet raises his voice, he sounds phony. And its characteristic hero is neither the 'Great Man' nor the romantic rebel, both doers of extraordinary deeds, but the man or woman in any walk of life who, despite all the impersonal pressures of modern society, manages to acquire and preserve a face of his own."

The critical statement of *The Dyer's Hand* is, for all the charm and beauty of the book, as austere as the muse herself. Criticism is as hard to make as poetry, and

> If good literary critics are rarer than good poets or novelists, one reason is the nature of human egotism. A poet or a novelist has to learn to be humble in the face of his subject matter which is life in general. But the subject matter of a critic, before which he has to learn to be humble, is made up of authors, that is to say, of human individuals, and this kind of humility is much harder to acquire. It is far easier to say—"Life is more important than anything I can say about it"—than to say—"Mr. A's work is more important than anything I can say about it."

The Dyer's Hand nevertheless deserves that tribute.

I Will Tell You About It
Because It Is Interesting

When he accepted the National Book Award last April for this enormous, enormously attractive and energetic book, A. R. Ammons sent the Committee some remarks that constitute an oblique definition of poetry. The subjectivity of his view of the art is striking:

> I'm very grateful that there is this thing called poetry which those dislocated into some extreme can attempt to engage and, by engaging, realize a center to their worlds and, better still, understand that their worlds relate to the world we all make and share.

That's pretty heavy stuff. The abstraction and the heft and the wisdom of it recur, sometimes brilliantly, sometimes heavy-footedly, throughout the book. But it is a viable definition, if it has launched and sustained this handsome and eccentric body of work. *Collected Poems 1951–1971* is a record of moments of total attention: outward toward the sensible world, inward to the dreams and moods of our solipsism, and fusing the two worlds in ways that heighten the reality of each. A little paradigm poem is called "Attention":

> Down by the bay I
> kept in mind
> at once
> the tips of all the rushleaves

Parnassus 1 (Fall–Winter 1973).

and so
came to know
balance's cost and true:
somewhere though in the whole field
is the one
tip
I will someday lose out of mind
and fall through.

The book is divided into four chronological sections which don't follow the sequences of the books they first appeared in but seem to intend some larger account of the poet's journey through the two decades, a diary of his intellectual and spiritual progress. There is a respectable tradition for the verse journal. Gary Snyder's *Earth House Hold* and Philip Whalen's *On Bear's Head* are two recent examples where pure character, and characteristic incident, create a unity and intensity of language that is very like poetry but remains, by and large, prose. Ammons's book is not like that; it is all poetry, if occasionally uneven. But it has a great consistency of character, too—almost the exasperating consistency of our greatest poet and the one whom, in range and curiosity, he most resembles:

They would not find me changed from him they knew—
Only more sure of all I thought was true.

It is in fact a character and an intelligence that remind you of Robert Frost: his patient, naturalist's eye in "Design," his curiosity about how things work in "Spring Pools," his *Scientific American* excitement about galaxies and molecules. Neither poet is afraid to think or generalize in verse (sometimes you wish they were). Here are two poems, each a little graceless by the poet's usual standards, about scientific mysteries as metaphors for human ones. Frost is writing about a geode struck into glowing by a cathode ray:

A head thrusts in as for the view,
But where it is it thrusts in from
Or what it is it thrusts into
By that Cyb'laean avenue,
And what can of its coming come,

And whither it will be withdrawn,
And what take hence or leave behind,
These things the mind has pondered on
A moment and still asking gone.
Strange apparition of the mind!

But the impervious geode
Was entered, and its inner crust
Of crystals with a ray cathode
At every point and facet glowed
In answer to the mental thrust.

Eyes seeking the response of eyes
Bring out the star, bring out the flowers.
Thus concentrating earth and skies
So none need be afraid of size.
All revelation has been ours.

("All Revelation")

Ammons writes about "Laser,"

An image comes
and the mind's light, confused
as that on surf
or ocean shelves,
gathers up,
parallelizes, focuses
and in a rigid beam illuminates the image:

the head seeks in itself
fragments of left-over light:
to cast a new
direction,
any direction,
to strike and fix
a random, contradicting image:

but any found image falls
back to darkness or
the lesser beams splinter and
go out:
the mind tries to
dream of diversity, of mountain
rapids shattered with sound and light.

of wind fracturing brush or
bursting out of order against a mountain
range: but the focused beam
folds all energy in:
the image glares filling all space:
the head falls and
hangs and cannot wake itself.

The other important concern he shares with Frost, I feel,
is a fascination with dialectics, the mysterious forces in the
universe that insist on having it both ways when we are hot
for certainties. Here are three fragments from Ammons's
"Essay on Poetics" which Frost (after tsk-tsking a little as I
will do now and then about the prosody) would have been
delighted with:

poems are arresting in two ways: they attract attention with
glistery astonishment and they hold it: stasis: they gather and
stay: the progression is from sound and motion to silence and
    rest.

(p. 310)*

        a white oak, for example—
it does not allow haphazard change to riddle it—no, it pro-
    tects the
species by the death of thousands of individuals: but lets the

species buy by the hazard of its individuals the capacity to
    adjust,
should adjustment be indicated or allowed: that is terrifying
    and
pleasing: a genetic cull myself, I have the right to both
    emotions.

(316–17)

    it's hard to say whether the distinguishers
or the resemblancers are sillier: they work with noumena
    every
day, but speak of the invisible to them and they laugh with

---

*Page references in parenthesis are from *Collected Poems*.

silver modernity: well, as I said, we are more certain that we
are about than what we are about:

(317)

The purview of the poems is all-embracing, like Whitman's:

    it is
    wonderful

        how things work: I will tell you
                about it
                because

    it is interesting
    and because whatever is
    moves in weeds
       and stars and spider webs
    and known
       is loved;
    in that love,
    each of us knowing it,
    I love you.

(114–15)

public, I have nothing to say to you, nothing: except,
look at the caterpillar under this clump of grass: it
is fuzzy: look at the sunset: it is colorful: listen:

it's hard to compete here in winter: snow makes the
broadest impression, and ineradicable eradication: slows
and muffles: you can hear the snow fall, a fizz: if

I cannot look at you, I can look with you: since there
is something between us, let it be a thing we share:

(363)

    Have you listened for the things I have left out?
    I am nowhere near the end yet and already
            hear
        the hum of omissions,

(90)

        Honor the maggot,
        supreme catalyst

> he spurs the rate of change:
> (all scavengers are honorable: I love them all
> will scribble hard as I can for them)

(110)

Pantheism runs thematically through the poems of natural observation, the poet identifying himself with the small and with the wind, like Roethke. (It wouldn't surprise me if all the poets I compare him with were favorites of Ammons's, though his unique, various voice always declares its own person):

> oh I will be addled and easy and move
> over this prairie in the wind's keep.
> long-lying sierras blue-low in the distance:
> I will glide and say little
> (what would you have me say? I know nothing;
> still, I cannot help singing)

(83)

Here is a characteristic poem from the first part of the book:

> The whaleboat struck
> and we came ashore
> to the painted faces
>   O primitives I said
> and the arrow sang to my throat
> Leaving myself on the shore
> I went away
> and when a heavy wind caught me I said
>   My body lies south
>   given over to vultures and flies
> and wrung my hands
> so the wind went on
> Another day a wind came saying
>   Bones
>   lovely and white
>   lie on the southern sand
>   the ocean has washed bright
> I said
>   O bones in the sun
> and went south

The flies were gone
The vultures no longer searched
the ends of my hingeless bones
for a trace of lean or gristle
Breathing the clean air
I picked up a rib
   to draw figures in the sand
till there is no roar in the ocean
no green in the sea
till the northwind flings no waves
across the open sea
I running in and out with the waves
I singing old Devonshire airs
                ("The Whaleboat Struck")

Ammons seems to me one of the surest craftsmen of organic form, the prosody found at the heart of the experience of the poem. I wish I knew how to demonstrate this judgment objectively, but I can only report that I find almost no mannerism or irritating arbitrariness of line structure in the whole 391 pages, except in three long poems I will presently take to task for their structural defects. Here I will cite some passages where, in the course of talking about prosody, the lines exemplify or act out his passive theory.

He seems to have three principle gambits for establishing line-structure. The first is a short, counter-rational line that has the effect of calling attention to individual words, and to arbitrary clusters of words, as if they were strange artifacts or *objets trouvés* of sound. This is the opening of a poem called "Motion."

The word is
not the thing:
is
a construction of,
a tag for,
the thing: the
word in
no way
resembles
the thing, except

as sound
resembles,
as in *whirr,*
sound:
the relation
between what this
as words
is
and what is
is tenuous: we
agree upon
this as the net to
cast on what
is: the finger
to
point with:

A second method is to phrase the poem in loose loops of
meaning, paying an easy attention to the units of sense. The
closing lines of "Corsons Inlet" exemplify and discuss that
freedom:

I see narrow orders, limited tightness, but will
not run to that easy victory:
   still around the looser, wider forces work:
   I will try
   to fasten into order enlarging grasps of disorder, widen-
      ing
scope but enjoying the freedom that
Scope eludes my grasp, that there is no finality of vision
that I have perceived nothing completely,
   that tomorrow a new walk is a new walk.

The third method is a kind of cookie-cutter. He counts lines
and sets them up in regular clusters, the lines themselves hav-
ing no predominant accent- or syllable-count though they are
often visually about of a length. The clusters of lines ordi-
narily don't correspond to divisions of meaning, nor do the
stanzas into which they are sometimes grouped. There are
some extremely good poems taken by this form. "World" and
"The Strait" are particularly elegant examples. But the follow-

ing lines are from a not particularly happy example of it and offer a not particularly exact simile, though original. "Hibernaculum" is written in, alas, 112 numbered 9-line stanzas:

> one thing poetry could be resembled to is
> soup: the high moving into clarity of quintessential
> consomme: then broth, the homogeneous cast of substance's
>
> shadow: then the falling out of diversity into specific
> identity, carrot cube, pea, rice grain: then the chunky
> predominance of beef hunk, long bean, in heavy gravy:
>
> (357)

Before leaving the subject of his line, I will quote not from the "Essay on Poetics," which I find formally unresolved, but a short poem called "Poetics" which tells perhaps as much as can be told about the mystery of form, and how to attend on it:

> I look for the way
> things will turn
> out spiraling from a center,
> the shape
> things will take to come forth in
>
> so that the birch tree white
> touched black at branches
> will stand out
> wind-glittering
> totally its apparent self:
>
> I look for the forms
> things want to come as
> from what black wells of possibility,
> how a thing will
> unfold:
>
> not the shape on paper—though
> that, too—but the
> uninterfering means on paper:
>
> not so much looking for the shape
> as being available
> to any shape that may be

summoning itself
through me
from self not mine but ours.

The three long poems that I feel are the least successful parts of the book come toward the end, in the most recent section. If they were brave or experimental, I wouldn't quarrel with their partial failure. But they don't seem to represent any new risks or to serve his talent in any new ways. Rather, they indulge in familiar and easy discourse, relying on their charm to cover up a certain aimlessness. All three contain short lyric runs that are quite worthy of Ammons's gift, but all three contain lapses of energy, dim places, failures of transition, that I can only ascribe to their not having found a clear organic structure. They read like catalogs, by a man whose best poems are journeys.

There are some 68 poems in the index of first lines that begin with "I," (not counting another couple of dozen starting "Today I," "Five years ago I," etc.) and mostly the plot of these poems is some excited narrative of the imagination, melding together seamlessly a chain of events not before melded. "Attention," the little poem quoted at the start of this review, is a short example, whereas an 82-line narrative about a day spent driving through New Jersey, "Batsto," is one of the longest, as though there was a kind of time-span or line-span that constituted a natural limit, for this poet, for this kind of poem.

In any case, a poem called "Summer Session" is too long a trip. It appears to be a perfectly autobiographical account of the poet-teacher's days during a summer term at Cornell, making dailiness and domesticity catalysts for eternal thoughts. Something in Ammons's process of association—so marvelously sure as to make poems like "Bridge" and "Motion for Motion" and "Visit" permanent additions to the language—is lacking here, and the language itself often suffers a dimming to soft prose. Perhaps the promiscuity of the six-week prose journal that it is presumably distilled from does not admit of the faithfulness of attention usual in his poems. The wit, which I think is meant to hold it together (and might do that for an audience of insiders), doesn't quite do so for an outsider. In the end, it is uncomfortably like the in-jokes of a New York School poet who has strayed to Lake Cayuga.

"Extremes and Moderations," 100 4-line stanzas with a short lyric, tipped in, is keyed even lower, ending with a line that takes on double meaning, "in an enclosure like earth's there's no place to dump stuff off." "Hibernaculum" concludes

> I'm reading Xenophon's *Oeconomicus* "with
> considerable pleasure and enlightenment" and with
> appreciation that saying so fills out this stanza nicely.
>
> (388)

The "Essay on Poetics" is another rambling poem in which I think I have identified eleven separate short poems. Separated, they would have the accuracy and energy of the normal Ammons lyric; strung together rather wilfully they make you aware of the conversational transitions, the lecturer's approach to ideas. The discovered, mysterious affinities that are Ammons's particular lyric strategy are shorted out between parts. "Extremes and Moderations" suggests at one point (humorously?) that an easy virtuosity informs the verse:

> constructing the stanza is not in my case exceedingly
> difficult
>
> (329)

but I don't find the versification any more consistent in these poems than the forward movement.

These four poems, although they seem to have a higher incidence of abstraction and generalization, are seldom dull and often very interesting, if only because Ammons is so bright and well-informed. It would not be honest or to the point to single out prosy passages. But *connectively* these long poems are unsatisfactory, in a context of a volume of shorter works whose special motion is that of the easy, natural connection of open metaphor. And as for the form, whether it is the slack freedom of "Summer Session" or the apparently orderly stanzas of the other three, it isn't up to Ammons's standards. In his best work, one thinks of the lines in Frost's "The Ax-

Helve" where the French-Canadian craftsman is demonstrating organic form in a metaphor out of the wood of trees, so dear to both poets:

> He showed me that the lines of a good helve
> Were native to the grain before the knife
> Expressed them, and its curves were no false curves
> Put on it from without. And there its strength lay
> For the hard work.

But the book survives these flaws as it will survive long, well-intentioned attempts to describe and praise it.

Every Poem an Epitaph

With reference to T. S. Eliot's poems, we seem now to stand at the point of their least usefulness. That hard instruction which in their novelty they had to impart has been received and made good use of. We have our new poetry, and what its founder said is now common knowledge or can be better learned from later and smoother practitioners. But we are not yet in a position to use Eliot's poems as a fixed point; we cannot evaluate the sensibility that came with them, just because that sensibility is our own, the common sensibility of contemporary poetry. That it is also a very strange sensibility, and therefore still harder to assess from where we stand, is witnessed by the estrangement between contemporary poetry and the average reader. Finally, I think we do not really use Eliot's poems because we do not understand them well, and therefore are not as much moved by them as we need to be for poems to be useful. At the moment, then, it is no longer a revelation, this poetry, and not yet a dogma, but less useful than either of those, it is a kind of custom with us.

At this moment in our dealings with Eliot a wave of destructive criticism, heralded by Robert Hillyer's irresponsible attack in the *Saturday Review of Literature* this June, is to be expected. There are many readers, surely, who in good faith have despaired of finding in Eliot's work the poetry that they have been told is there, and who would willingly be absolved, by some authority, of the responsibility of reading such difficult verse. What is needed to hearten these readers is the present book by Elizabeth Drew, which is an honest and sensitive attempt to further a general understanding of Eliot's poems.

In her study of Eliot's major poems, Miss Drew has accomplished a task which I think none of the previous critical studies has done, the task of demonstrating how Eliot's major poems are related, or are, in fact, all of a piece. Other discussions of the unity of Eliot's poetry have perhaps *asserted* as much, and skillful readers may have recognized the very unity Miss Drew uncovers, but for this reader the unity had always appeared a trifle mechanical, a matter of recurrent images, references and attitudes rather than of a constant *intention*. In this book Elizabeth Drew seems to have discovered, by a means which will strike many as extremely dubious, almost the exact history of the sensibility behind the poems. This history not only accommodates satisfactorily the incremental repetitions mentioned above, but also elucidates remarkably the total meanings of individual poems.

Readers who, like myself, have bogged down repeatedly at the task of holding together the longer poems as they read them, and who have in consequence taken to reading Eliot as a collection of short lyric passages of varying degrees of satisfaction, will be astonished at how the parts assemble themselves. By the joint prophecy of Jung and Miss Drew, these bones live.

Miss Drew's method, and do not be put off until you have seen how discreetly it is used, is to make a Jungian case history of Eliot's imagery. In the preface she gives and takes fair warning about the method:

> I have found what is, to me, an interesting parallel in symbolic content between the progression of dream symbols described by Jung as arising during what he calls "the integration of the personality" (and which he relates to the history of myth), and some of those appearing in Eliot's poetry during the course of its development. But this is not a book about rival schools of psychology and anthropology. . . . Psychology can suggest a good deal about the unconscious forces at work behind the conception of art, but it has limitations which make it a very poor critical instrument. It cannot touch the work of art itself, and it cannot distinguish between good art and bad art. . . .

There has, however, been no attempt to write of the body of [Eliot's] poetry as a process of growth, as an "integration of the personality." The particular purpose of this book is to do that, and to help the general reader, and the student, to a fuller enjoyment of the individual poems by analysis and discussion.

Miss Drew's analyses and discussions proceed by the familiar pattern of paraphrase and cross-reference, usually up to the point where the total intellectual meaning of some larger division is in doubt. There, habitually, she turns to the design of Jung's archetypal imagery and sets that up beside Eliot. In "Marina," for example, dealing with the lines:

> Bowsprit cracked with ice and paint cracked with heat.
> I made this, I have forgotten
> And remember.
> The rigging weak and the canvas rotten
> Between one June and another September.
> Made this unknowing, half conscious, unknown, my own.
> The garboard strake leaks, the seams need caulking.
> This form, this face, this life
> Living to live in a world of time beyond me; let me
> Resign my life for this life, my speech for that unspoken,
> The awakened, lips parted, the hope, the new ships.

she writes:

> Then with all the unaccountable pattern of dream, we hear of the strange ship whose bow the water is lapping. The sea-world and the dream-world meet. Pericles and Marina are together on this very insecure and dilapidated vessel which seems quite out of keeping with the perfection of the experience. But the significance of it is in the "I made this."

Then she quotes:

> As a human construction, the ship has the meaning (in the dream sequence of "transformation") of a system, method or way. Jung, *Integration of the Personality*, p. 189.

116

Again, dealing with the trees in *Ash-Wednesday*, she derives her solution from this quotation from the same work:

> The appearance of trees as images, says Jung, are often "intermediate symbols" in the general archetype of transformation. They represent "rootedness, repose and growth . . . as also the union of sky and earth."

This recourse to Jung's patterns is not limited to specific parallels of imagery. The total experience of the "integration of the personality" is invoked, with the thesis that Eliot, like every major artist, accomplishes this experience anew for his own time. Miss Drew describes this pattern at one point in these terms:

> It is the experience of detachment from the world of objective reality as the centre of existence and the finding of "a new dimension" in which it can and must be contemplated and lived. Detachment too from the ego as the centre of interest and the discovery of a different centre. As such it involves the process of the death of an old life and the birth of a new, the process traced back by Frazer and other scholars as the inner meaning of the symbolism of the oldest Fertility rituals, and the basis of their development into tragic drama.

Because this integration is a protracted process, accomplished with great difficulty, Miss Drew does not look for the complete pattern in any one work, unless perhaps in *Four Quartets*. Rather, elements of the pattern appear throughout the poems. In the early poems, "Prufrock" and the Sweeney poems, for example, she finds chiefly the discontent with the "world of objective reality as the centre of existence." By the time of *The Waste Land* the destruction of the old self and old life has reached its most savage state, but no location of a new center has been reached. In *Ash-Wednesday* there has been found the conviction of the existence of a new center, and the imagery deals with the withdrawal from the old; the new conviction is seen positively in the "recognition scenes" of the three "Ariel" poems, and negatively in the satiric attack of "Coriolan" on man-centered cultures. In *Four Quartets*, where growth and modification of symbols occurs on a large scale within one work, Miss Drew finds that both detachment and relatedness, both birth and death, are reconciled and their natures revealed. The final symbols of the poem are shown also to be the final symbols of the "integration" pattern.

The value of this approach to the poems, apart from suggesting a number of valid readings for obscure passages, is that it accounts for the changing values which certain symbols have for Eliot in different poems. The values of symbols, in this scheme, change as the personality progresses through the stages of its transformation: the sea in "Prufrock" may be an escape to innocence; in *The Waste Land* water is the murderous refreshment of that which must drown to find life; while in "The Dry Salvages" water is both of those (no meaning is ever *revoked* from a symbol, but only added to and modified) and also a symbol of the race history and the vehicle of our faring forward.

Read in this light, not just images but whole poems can be seen to modify their predecessors—as Eliot puts it, every poem an epitaph. We can also understand better by this approach than by another why the middle poems, in particular, are in an essential way incomplete, and why it is possible for two competent critics to disagree as to whether *The Waste Land* ends in hope or despair; there was simply no image of resolution yet.

Miss Drew plods a good deal, but she avoids, it seems to me, the presumptions to which such an undertaking as this is liable. She approaches Eliot's states of belief and affection only through his printed work, and only with her avowed intention, to elucidate the poems. She does not force her theory, and indeed at the end of the book you can dismiss all of the Jungian parallels without losing the value of her exegesis. In the course of the work there are several specific errors in reading, and occasionally (like Brooks and Mathiessen here) she goes a long way to bring back a reading, *any* reading, for an obscure passage. She is less satisfactory than Cleanth Brooks on *The Waste Land,* and adds little to his essay. On the "Ariel" poems, "Coriolan" and *Four Quartets,* she is at her best.

If Miss Drew's book does as much as I have said to increase the understanding of Eliot's poems, it also exposes abruptly the incompleteness and partial failure of each of them. The large body of criticism and explication which these poems have required and annexed to themselves tell against them as useable poems. In requiring such paraphernalia, Eliot's work is unlike both good art and good myth. While the meaning of myths tends to be hidden or at least ambiguous, there is always a level of narrative meaning which is clear enough to give the symbols a surface life of their own. We are not in doubt as to *what is going on,* yet we sense that beneath the clear dramatic surface is another level, complete with all its meaningful ambiguities. In Eliot's poems, the mystery in the depths is sometimes quite lost in a mystery on the surface; how can we ponder what a poem *means,* unless we can tell what it *says?* For what it says, we rely on a surface life given the poems by critics like Miss Drew.

Eliot has failed to objectify the imagery which the critics are called upon to solve. His failure to do this is due, I think, not to any theoretical misconception of the nature of poetry, but to a deficiency of sensibility. He has familiarized himself so thoroughly with the myths and symbols of our culture that these have a life and meaning for him that is unique; but it has cost him his feeling for what of all this is communicating, and what is not. A very significant and dynamic thing about our culture, the area of its ignorance, is evidently not known to him or respected as a vital force.

This insensitivity to the communicative force of symbols would be less serious if it were not re-enforced by another deviation from the norm in Eliot: his theory of poetry has insisted, largely for historical reasons, on the irrational nature of poetic communication. He has, I believe unnecessarily, chosen to emphasize this truth by eliminating rational transition and structure from his poems. There are readers of Eliot who deny the conjunction of these two errors, and others who say they are unimportant. Surely the work of Miss Drew atones for something. It is a measure of Eliot's power as a poet that such labors, on the part of critic and readers, continue to be felt rewarding.

A Steady Storm
of Correspondences:
Theodore Roethke's Long Journey
Out of the Self

Criticism, when it is attentive and appreciative, is a record of one man's encounter with the enduring personality of another. When Eliot said that poetry is not the expression of a personality but an escape from it, I think he meant that our human personalities are clumsy and inexact and that the poet creates another, more deliberate character for himself in his poems. In any case, that is what I understand Roethke to have meant by his life work.

His published work, from *Open House* through *The Far Field*, creates one of those unmistakable human identities that make up the tradition of English poetry. They are of all sizes but, like the carp in an imperial pond, do not eat one another, being sacred. Some are austere or eccentric and others we may simply not like. But all the writers who go on concerning us after their deaths are men and women who have escaped from a confused human identity into the identity they willed and consented to.

It seems sometimes to be casually assumed that it is harder to bring off an enduring artistic accomplishment today than in the past. This is probably one of our harmless provincialisms: the statistics suggest that it has always been next to im-

In *Theodore Roethke: Essays on the Poetry*, edited by Arnold Stein (University of Washington Press, 1965).

possible. In every time there are a few who shape their work—*instead of their lives,* it may seem—with a ruthless perfection. The intellect of man is forced to choose perfection of the life, or of the work, Yeats put it. Such work as the artist chooses is a door that must be unlocked deliberately, and I think of the boy in the fairy tale who cuts a key from the flesh of his own finger because he has no other substance. I can't feel that the twentieth century has been ingenious enough to make this job any harder. The poetry of Theodore Roethke is as remarkable for its deliberate movement toward a goal as for the success that attends it on its way.

The poems in *Open House,* his first book, not published until he was thirty-three, were marked by an elegance that was more than formal. The subjects were not tame—from the outset Roethke must have sensed that the genius inhabiting him was uncouth—but the issues of the poems were resolved by poetic formulas. The first of his recurrent poems about the discomfort of wearing flesh, for instance, concludes with these lines:

> Yet such is my unseemliness:
> I hate my epidermal dress,
> The savage blood's obscenity,
> The rags of my anatomy,
> And willingly would I dispense
> With false accouterments of sense,
> To sleep immodestly, a most
> Incarnadine and carnal ghost.
>
> ("Epidermal Macabre")

It's a pretty conceit, verbally very pretty, but you feel that part of the emotion has been lopped off to make it come out like a proper metaphysical poem, that it is, in fact, an inaccurate statement from a man who will later say things like "The flesh can make the spirit visible" and

> I teach my eyes to hear, my ears to see
> How body from spirit slowly does unwind
> Until we are pure spirit at the end.
>
> ("Infirmity")

—certainly a more complex and affectionate vision of the flesh.

It seems to have been the aesthetic premise of the first book that poetry is obliged to set experience in order. In the little poem called "The Bat," notice not only the smoothness of the metrics—smooth to the point of unfeeling—but also the orderly summary at the end.

> By day the bat is cousin to the mouse.
> He likes the attic of an aging house.
>
> His fingers make a hat about his head.
> His pulse beat is so slow we think him dead.
>
> He loops in crazy figures half the night
> Among the trees that face the corner light.
>
> But when he brushes up against a screen,
> We are afraid of what our eyes have seen:
>
> For something is amiss or out of place
> When mice with wings can wear a human face.

The suggestiveness of "We are afraid of what our eyes have seen," a line that throws the reader back on his own resources of fright, as good spookery does, is dispelled by the sheer tidiness of the last couplet that tells how and why to be afraid.

One of the most successful short lyrics in *Open House* is called "Mid-Country Blow." Here the experience itself is beautifully articulate and cleanly defined; it is not, therefore, diminished by the perfection of form and image with which it is realized. But what is striking about it, all these years later, is that it is not recognizably a Roethke poem at all. If someone told you it was by Robert Frost or Richard Wilbur, you might believe him—you could compare it with "Bereft" by one or with "Pity" by the other sooner than with one of the greenhouse poems.

> All night and all day the wind roared in the trees,
> Until I could think there were waves rolling high as
>   my bedroom floor;
> When I stood at the window, an elm bough swept to my
>   knees;
> The blue spruce lashed like a surf at the door.

The second dawn I would not have believed:
The oak stood with each leaf stiff as a bell.
When I looked at the altered scene, my eye was undeceived,
But my ear still kept the sound of the sea like a shell.

Open House was, in fact, a stylish apprentice work. Like Frost's *A Boy's Will*, we return to it more because of what comes out of it than what was in it. We can admire a certain doggedness with which Roethke runs through his excercises in the genres of the forties. The poem called "Sale," for instance, which presents the decline of a great family in terms of an auction, is in the style of W. H. Auden's satires, the style that inspired a lot of Karl Shapiro's first book published a year later. The tag line of each stanza is set off by a dash, to nudge us with the fashionable irony. The book is full of order, but it is mostly the order of artifice.

The Lost Son and Other Poems was published seven years later, in 1948. It projects unmistakably the character of an original poet. Even of the three poems that Roethke removed from the volume in subsequent collections, only one could conceivably be by anybody else: a skillful but slightly modish poem called "Double Feature," and this is no exercise but only a poem less sure in its persona than the others. The middle stanza is not quite in character:

I dawdle with groups near the rickety pop-corn stand;
Dally at shop windows, still reluctant to go;
I teeter, heels hooked on the curb, scrape a toe;
Or send off a car with vague lifts of a hand.

If that is out of character it is because this is the book of the greenhouse poems—"the book I continue to think of as the great one," his friend Stanley Kunitz wrote the summer Roethke died. The greenhouse poems—just to name them is to conjure a fierce vegetable kingdom: "Cuttings," "Root Cellar," "Carnations," and the greatest one, inserted here later, "Frau Bauman, Frau Schmidt, and Frau Schwartze." They are themselves examples of vegetable energy, they spill over into Roethke's first free verse, every line of which seems as certain

of its shape as an opening leaf. Roethke is one of the few poets
whose internal rhyme and assonance is worth thinking about.
This poem seems to be the product of an ear attentive to every
sort of order that can be found in exact speech.

> That hump of a man bunching chrysanthemums
> Or pinching-back asters, or planting azaleas,
> Tamping and stamping dirt into pots,—
> How he could flick and pick
> Rotten leaves or yellow petals,
> Or scoop out a weed close to flourishing roots,
> Or make the dust buzz with a light spray,
> Or drown a bug in one spit of tobacco juice,
> Or fan life into wilted sweet-peas with his hat,
> Or stand all night watering roses, his feet blue in rubber
>   boots.

("Old Florist")

There is a bigger aesthetic premise at work in this book, the
premise that is to lead Roethke through the restless course of
his work. Instead of ordering experience, these poems attend
on experience with the conviction that there is order in it.
However imperfectly his eye might see it or his voice might
articulate it—and he went on writing occasional shapeless
lines and passages all his life—this *revealed* order was the only
one Roethke served from this time on. It led him to write
some formless and unsuccessful poems, but it led through
them to one of the affirmative bodies of work of his genera-
tion, and one of the most perceptive.

Along with the new freedom of form in this book, perhaps
underlying it, is a freedom of association, an openness to meta-
phorical suggestion, and the fearful possibility, entertained to
the last moment, that an order inimical to man's spirit might
be discovered, or no order at all. More and more of the state-
ments praise a wise and attentive passiveness, the attitude that
was to flower in one of his final poems in the refrain, "The
right thing happens to the happy man."

The second of the two poems called "Cuttings" moves by
this trust in association. (I might say first that I think it is one

of a great many poems that can be damaged by overt sexual interpretation. Insofar as we are sexual beings—and happily that is quite far—things lurk in our minds. But insofar as a skillful artist speaks of experience other than the sexual, we must suppose that he intends to treat other experience, and pay attention to that.)

> This urge, wrestle, resurrection of dry sticks,
> Cut stems struggling to put down feet,
> What saint strained so much,
> Rose on such lopped limbs to a new life?
>
> I can hear, underground, that sucking and sobbing,
> In my veins, in my bones I feel it,—
> The small waters seeping upward,
> The tight grains parting at last.
> When sprouts break out,
> Slippery as fish,
> I quail, lean to beginnings, sheath-wet.
>
> ("Cuttings, *later*")

The acceptance of disturbing and disorderly associations, and of the formal risks appropriate to them, culminates in four long poems at the end of *The Lost Son*. These were to be, in fact, the beginnings of another book somewhat the way a long poem called "Burnt Norton" was to lead its author into a larger scheme. Three years later Roethke published *Praise to the End!* and placed the four poems where they are, if not less obscure, at least better sustained by other poems. But the title poem, "The Lost Son," appears first of these four in the earlier book.

It is not an easy poem, yet the obscurity is that of a lucid dream, where only the causes and connections, not the facts or events, are in doubt. The causes seem to be the death of parents, the speaker's recognition of his aloneness, sealed off in his link of the chain of human life, and the loss of childhood and its illusion of order. The fourth section is another greenhouse poem and comes to its climax as the child's eyes see the father, the greenhouse keeper, arriving as a figure of beautiful and terrible order:

> Once I stayed all night.
> The light in the morning came slowly over the white
> Snow.
> There were many kinds of cool
> Air.
> Then came steam.
>
> Pipe-knock.
>
> Scurry of warm over small plants.
> Ordnung! Ordnung!
> Papa is coming!

Another of these four poems, "A Field of Light," stands alone in a recent anthology and is in fact a self-contained lyric poem of slightly more than average difficulty. It treats a child's vision of the world, not always with a child's vocabulary, and is reminiscent of Dylan Thomas's "Fern Hill" but without Thomas's preoccupation with time. A few lines at the end convey its grace:

> Listen, love,
> The fat lark sang in the field;
> I touched the ground, the ground warmed by the killdeer,
> The salt laughed and the stones;
> The ferns had their ways, and the pulsing lizards,
> And the new plants, still awkward in their soil,
> The lovely diminutives.
>
> I could watch! I could watch!
> I saw the separateness of all things!
> My heart lifted up with the great grasses;
> The weeds believed me, and the nesting birds.
> There were clouds making a rout of shapes crossing a wind-
>   break of cedars,
> And a bee shaking drops from a rain-soaked honeysuckle.
> The worms were delighted as wrens.
> And I walked, I walked through the light air;
> I moved with the morning.

These poems are later placed in the vague narrative of *Praise to the End!*, the hardest of Roethke's books to read and very likely the hardest to write. I suppose it must also finally be accounted the least successful, but it commands admiration as a feat of exploration. At this point in Roethke's life (and if I were to guess at autobiographical events, I would guess that his recurrent mental illness—a humiliating and terrifying thing, surely, to a man of his imagination—acted in unison with his natural daring) he performed an experiment as brave and pigheaded as *The Waste Land.* He seems to have trusted his poetic voice to speak for itself, to have given control of the poems to his subconscious the way a ouija-board player gives his mind to the never-mind. And this seems not to have been a desperate move, the act of a man who had run dry in a certain vein, but rather the urge of an explorer who is led on by an unfolding continent, who may die landless, like Daniel Boone, but will have seen on the far side of the hills.

What Roethke does in *Praise to the End!* may be compared, again, to what Robert Lowell did in his *Life Studies,* which started in the prose piece—to my mind greatly inferior to the poems it begot—called "91 Revere Street." The two poets explore and identify them*selves,* the self being the intermediary of all experience, in a way that it is possible for people of a certain wholeness to do without egotism. In Roethke's case, what he found was a poetic myth as durable as Yeats's, though humbler. His humbler poetic talent was to live off the revelation of this book for the rest of its natural life in much the way that Yeats's poetry can be said to have lived off *A Vision.*

Praise to the End! is an anatomy of Roethke's imagery and sensibility. In the course of recounting a spiritual autobiography he tells us what he feels about cats and dogs, hot and cold, father and mother, trees, weeds, birds, stones, and fish, and about his special image, the wind. He goes over and over them until he gets them right. The instrument of enquiry is a primitive one, the feelings of childhood. At a later time, when he has returned from this exploration and resumed the use of symmetrical forms, he will write in a villanelle, "We think by feeling. What is there to know?" *Praise to the End!* completes the process of casting off artificial form in favor of the organic. The book is a continuous feeling out of the structure of existence in contempt, or near contempt, of reason. Toward the end of the book the speaker says:

> Reason? That dreary shed, that hutch for grubby schoolboys!
> The hedgewren's song says something else.
> I care for a cat's cry and the hugs, live as water.
> I've traced these words in sand with a vestigial tail;
> Now the gills are beginning to cry.
> Such a sweet noise: I can't sleep for it.
> Bless me and the maze I'm in!
> Hello, thingy spirit.
>
> ("I Cry, Love! Love!")

Knowledge is *felt;* and this last passage suggests that the senses by which we accumulate it are prehuman and that human speech is as instinctive as that of the other creatures. There are a couple of interesting consequences of this position in the poems, repeated patterns of syntax that imply that our speech is primarily involuntary, an animal cry. One of these is a series of soft invocations, sometimes the address of a vulnerable creature to implacable forces, more often a fraternal appeal to the mercy of little things. The following are in their order in the poems but occur at least a poem apart. They are all given urgency by assonance or consonance or alliteration.

> God, give me a near, I hear flowers.
>
> Whisper me over, / Why don't you, begonia,
>
> Hear me, soft ears and roundy stones!
>
> Leaves, do you like me any?
>
> Soothe me, great groans of underneath, . . .

There are a number of other askings like these, but two that occur in "The Lost Son" are particularly explicit. The poem opens with a section called "The Flight" which deals with death:

> At Woodlawn I heard the dead cry:
> I was lulled by the slamming of iron. . . .
> I shook the softening chalk of my bones,

Saying,
Snail, snail, glister me forward,
Bird, soft-sigh me home.
Worm, be with me.
This is my hard time.

The third section, "The Gibber," contains these three lines:

What a small song. What slow clouds. What dark water.
Hath the rain a father? All the caves are ice. Only the snow's
    here.
I'm cold. I'm cold all over. Rub me in father and mother.

These little prayers suggest the vulnerability of childhood and
also the serious, irrational voice in which we talk to ourselves.
It seems to me that these poems convey the act of talking to
oneself as well as "The Love Song of J. Alfred Prufrock" does.

The other pattern of syntax that is repeated fairly often is a
sort of parody of the folk saying, a two-part proposition that
sounds profound but frequently makes no rational sense at
all:

A tongue without song
            —Can still whistle in a jug.

Who reads in bed
            —Fornicates on the stove

The second pair of lines above is followed by this: "What a
whelm of proverbs, Mr. Pinch!" and just before another set
he says, "Dazzle me, dizzy aphorist, / Fling me a precept." I
think these passages are a self-challenge. The technique of
Praise to the End! has been to set down side by side, and
without rational connectives, short, stark declarations of fact
and questions with apparently irrelevant answers. These
mock-aphorisms, thrown in at intervals, have the effect of
calling into question the whole project: can knowledge be
worded, once it has been felt? They do this by reminding us
of the mindlessness of most human speech:

Time for the flat-headed man. I recognize that listener,
Him with the platitudes and rubber doughnuts,

> Melting at the knees, a varicose horror.
> Hello, hello. My nerves knew you, dear boy.
> ("The Shape of the Fire")

But whether I have solved these patterns correctly or not, they are phrasings to which he reverted, in intensity and perplexity, for the rest of his career. In *The Far Field* we find them both: "Leaves, leaves, lean forth and tell me what I am," he asks in "The Sequel," and in "The Longing," the turgid opening poem of the posthumous collection, he vexes himself:

> To this extent I'm a stalk.
> —How free; how all alone.
> Out of these nothings
> —All beginnings come.

Praise to the End! is a gazetteer of Roethke's country, naming the places where his feelings reside. Sometimes he is a tree. In separate poems these lines appear:

> When I stand, I'm almost a tree.

> Believe me, knot of gristle, I bleed like a tree
> I dream of nothing but boards

> I've more veins than a tree.

> Is he a bird or a tree? Not everyone can tell.

Sometimes he is a dog:

> Call off the dog, my paws are gone.

> I can't laugh at a procession of dogs.

> Up over a viaduct I came, to the snakes and sticks of another
>   winter,
> A two-legged dog hunting a new horizon of howls.

> I've crawled from the mire, alert as a saint or a dog.

The poems return to chosen words by the circling motion of the bug on a ouija board trying to find what it means. "Is circularity such a shame?" he asks in one poem. The most frequently repeated theme is the wind. It is named at least once in every poem. Later the collected poems would be called *Words for the Wind,* as though that were the chief of the powers he would propitiate. The wind seems to mean to him another self, all the trouble and delight of the world's weather, a witch-like white goddess who is his muse in a wordless existence, man's merciful destiny—more than one would suppose a word could be charged with.

Praise to the End!, although its prosody is less formal than any of Roethke's other books, shows a considerable variety of formal effects. The most strictly controlled are a series of nonsense rhymes that catch the tone of a child's voice making up language:

> Mips and ma the mooly moo,
> The likes of him is biting who,
> A cow's a care and who's a coo?—
> What footie does is final.
>
> ("Praise to the End!")

This is not unlike what Joyce does on the first page of the *Portrait of the Artist as a Young Man:* "Once upon a time and a very good time it was there was a moocow coming down along the road and this moocow along the road met a nicens little boy named baby Tuckoo."

The freest effect is a passage in the final poem which is set as prose and begins:

> And now are we to have that pelludious Jesus-shimmer over all things, the animal's candid gaze, a shade less than feathers, light's broken speech revived, a ghostly going of tame bears, a bright moon on gleaming skin, a thing you cannot say to whisper and equal a Wound?

The word "pelludious" I do not find in the dictionary, and the whole brief passage is, I think, a representation of the state of fear that arises in fear for one's own reason. It is the state that Joyce represents later in the *Portrait* during Stephen's religious crisis:

. . . Faces were there; eyes; they waited and watched.

—We knew perfectly well of course that although it was bound
to come to light he would find considerable difficulty in en-
deavoring to try to induce himself to try to endeavor to ascer-
tain the spiritual plenipotentiary and so we knew perfectly well
of course. . . .

The difference between Joyce and Roethke in both these cases
includes a broader humor in Roethke, humor that accompa-
nies most of the terror in his poems and is driven off only by
the tenderness.

Some years after *Praise to the End!*, Roethke wrote of his
formal purposes: "I have tried to transmute and purify my
'life,' the sense of being defiled by it, and, latterly, in longer
poems which try in their rhythms to catch the very movement
of the mind itself." He wrote these longer poems at intervals
for the rest of his career, knowing their risks. At least two
poems in *The Far Field*—"The Longing" and "The Abyss"—
seem to me seriously marred by the rhythmic meander of the
bemused mind. In "The Abyss," we know for sure that
Roethke knows his trouble:

> Be with me, Whitman, maker of catalogues:
> For the world invades me again,
> And once more the tongues begin babbling.
> And the terrible hunger for objects quails me. . . .
>
> Too much reality can be a dazzle, a surfeit;
> Too close immediacy an exhaustion. . . .

If in *Praise to the End!* and from time to time forever after
he flirted with the slow rhythm of chaos, it was part of the
deliberate identification we are concerned with. Immediately
after this volume, the poems clear like a brook. The natural
world returns as though a warped mirror had been made
straight. We recognize the images but they have cast off their
grotesques and difficulties, and the rhythms, even of the free
verse, become more musical. The "Elegy for Jane" comes
from this period. The imagery moves from animal to vegeta-
ble to elemental without confusion, conveying the lovely vital-

ity and changeableness of the dead girl. The rhythms of the irregular unrhymed lines are a demonstration, as so many of Roethke's free verse poems have been, of Pound's remark: "I think there is a 'fluid' as well as a 'solid' content, that some poems may have form as a tree has form, some as water poured into a vase." In the final volume there are some great, scraggly trees but they accommodate one of the great natural forces, a man's feeling.

It was perhaps because Roethke felt he had won through to a sure identity that in his later poems he made free to borrow meters, cadences, tones from other poets, but chiefly from Yeats. Once he seems to have been annoyed at some sly critic who discovered what he thought he had made obvious, for he wrote a little essay called "How to Write Like Somebody Else." In the course of it he says, "I suggest the central problem remains: whether a poem has been created." He quotes T. S. Eliot (a poet I believe he never liked): ". . . bad poets imitate; good poets steal," and adds, "In other words, take what you will with authority and see that you give it another, or even better life, in the new context."

I think it must be admitted that the influence of Yeats is too strong for Roethke in several of the published poems. There are lines and whole stanzas in which the rhetorical identity of Yeats—which is no mean identity—is stronger than the sensible identity, the identity of sensibility, of Roethke. Yet it is hard to think of another instance where a first-rate poet engaged so personally and in maturity a talent greater than his own. It is characteristic of Roethke. He knew he had tremendous authority in the sense that he uses the word in the essay, and it was characteristic that he wanted to match it against his master.

He speaks too, in this essay, of a technical difference between his verse and Yeats's.

> In the pentameter, I end-stop almost every line. . . . This is not necessarily a virtue—indeed from many points of view it is a limitation. But it is part of an effort, however clumsy, to bring the language back to bare, hard, even terrible statement. All this Yeats, himself a bowerbird if there ever was one, would have understood, and, possibly, approved.

Ordnung! Ordnung! Papa is coming!

It is always an interesting contest. In most of the Yeatsian poems Roethke's character—alternately tenderer, more blustering, and more humorous than Yeats's—makes a new thing of what he steals. But here is a stanza from a poem called "The Pure Fury" where I think the influence is not digested.

> The pure admire the pure, and live alone;
> I love a woman with an empty face.
> Parmenides put Nothingness in place;
> She tries to think, and it flies loose again.
> How slow the changes of a golden mean:
> Great Boehme rooted all in Yes and No;
> At times my darling squeaks in pure Plato.

Against this must be set a dozen perfect poems where something from Yeats has been transformed into a new thing: his ancestor poem has become "Otto," his meditative poem becomes "In a Dark Time," his poet poem becomes "Heard in a Violent Ward":

> In heaven, too,
> You'd be institutionalized.
> But that's all right,—
> If they let you eat and swear
> With the likes of Blake,
> And Christopher Smart,
> And that sweet man, John Clare.

The character that the work of Roethke presents seems to me as finished and distinct as any of his generation, perhaps matched only by Robert Lowell and John Berryman. What he does with it is both simpler and more affirmative than the work of those two men. Affirmations of any size are the great challenge of the artist. It is easier to achieve an identity, to see a unique vision, through misgivings, grievances, despair, on the one hand, or through utopias, sentimental optimisms, on the other. Only a very large and assured artist can retain his sense of self while deferring to created order. But created order, revealed order, is the source of the great visions of art. The artist looks at the world to affirm what is there, to affirm *he knows not what,* until his work is done. He risks this homelessness:

> I sing the wind around
> And hear myself return
> To nothingness, alone.
> The loneliest thing I know
> Is my own mind at play.
>
> ("His Foreboding")

And in the end it is because we see the man clearly that we are able to see with his eyes. The refrain of the earlier villanelle, "We learn by going where we have to go," yielded finally the refrain of the late one: "The right thing happens to the happy man." This is the man Theodore Roethke worked fifty-five years to perfect.

Notebook 1967–68

Complex and imperfect, like most of the accomplishments of serious men and women today, Robert Lowell's *Notebook 1967–68* is nevertheless a beautiful and major work. In what seems a propitiatory act to the modern god of chaos, the poet offers an account of his personal history as it has painstakingly ordered itself in images. It is the response of a racked but magnanimous mind, the response of a poet.

Lowell's work originally commanded attention because, among other virtues, it ranged over more human experience more generously than is common in modern poetry. Often the poet identified himself with people who had made historical errors, or with an artist who watched and understood such errors. His first major poem, "The Quaker Graveyard in Nantucket," goes beyond the conventional purposes of a wartime elegy for a dead sailor, to reckon up man's religious failures. Some years later when he made a secular reckoning in the title poem of *For the Union Dead* (1964), it was with the same sense of his own involvement.

In *Life Studies* (1959), the accounts of his family and of himself rise above the usual confessional poem in two respects. They are social criticism of the America they take place in, and they make serious moral judgments in which all the characters, including the speaker, share. Lowell's translations, which include dramatic versions of Racine, Aeschylus, Hawthorne, and Melville, and the wide range of lyrics in *Imitations* (1961), sometimes distort their originals in order to give the

New York Times Book Review, June, 1969. Copyright © 1969 by The New York Times Company. Reprinted by permission.

new works an imaginative impact intended for an earlier time. The *Notebook* extends in surprising but not illogical ways some of these thrusts from earlier work.

Many of the events in the *Notebook* are drawn from our common history of recent months, our wars and demonstrations, our assassinations and riots. Others are intensely, even hermetically, private. But throughout burns a passionate intelligence, a conscience, which the reader feels is trustworthy. After the worst has been said, it can still mete out praise, it is accountable for blame. "In truth I seem to have felt mostly the joys of living; in remembering, in recording, thanks to the gift of the Muse, it is the pain," Lowell says at the end of the book.

It is a big book, two and a half times the length of *Lord Weary's Castle,* the book that won Lowell a Pulitzer Prize in 1947, and we are asked to regard it as a single poem, though it is divided into self-contained stanzas with individual titles. "My meter, fourteen line unrhymed blank verse, is fairly strict at first and elsewhere, but often corrupts in single lines to the freedom of prose. Even with this license, I fear I have failed to avoid the themes and gigantism of the sonnet."

If he does largely avoid those weary assets of the sonnet, it is because his stanzas create their own decorum, a sequence of freely expanding images:

Stalin

Winds on the stems make them creak like things made by
    man;
a hedge of vines and bushes—three or four
kinds, grape leaf, elephant ear and alder,
an arabesque, imperfect and alive,
a hundred hues of green, the darkest shades
short of black, the palest leaf-backs far from white.
The state, if we could see behind the walls,
is woven of perishable vegetation.
Stalin? What shot him clawing up the tree of power—
millions plowed under like the crops they grew,
his intimates dying like the spider-bridegroom?
The large stomach could only chew success. What raised him
was the usual lust to break the icon,
joke cruelly, seriously, and be himself.

The movement here is from six lines of observed, wind-blown foliage, through two lines where that foliage becomes a rational metaphor for the state, into six final lines, where, with no pretext of rational transition, we are given the anthropoid figure of Stalin ravaging an allegorical landscape. This is a usual movement in the *Notebook* (not new to Lowell's work, but more systematic here than before)—a shuttling between the reporter's view and the mystic's, at an erratic pace designed to surprise us into binocular vision. "I lean heavily to the rational, but am devoted to surrealism," he tells us in a prose "Afterthought."

His form is flexible, but it has the strength to contain not only this freedom of image but the free association of events which constitutes his plot. A notebook's continuity is simply the fabric of the writer's attentions and concerns. Its chronology is as quick as thought and as confusing as history. "My plot rolls with the seasons," Lowell says. "The separate poems and actions are opportunist and inspired by impulse." In these conditions, the unit of articulation, the stanza-poem, creates a steady, rational reference.

As if to underscore this structure, many sections are pulled together by a line or two of commanding energy—dramatic, rhetorical, metaphoric. These conclusions are commonly the reverse of the quiet dying-away of a Shakespearean couplet. They are an intense cutting-off, often too dense syntactically to survive quotation. But here are several excerptable ones that bring the long poem to moments of temporary repose. I point to these lines not as samples of Lowell's lyric virtuosity— the book is shot through with that—but to make the point that in the torrent of events and images, these resolutions occur regularly. The stanzas are the stabilizing element, and lines like these delineate the stanzas:

> The king is laughing, all his men are killed,
> he is shaken by the news, as well he might be.

> In the days of the freeze, we see a minor sun,
> our winter moon bled for the solar rose.

> fame, a bouquet in the niche of forgetfulness!

Cattle have guts, but after the barn is burned,
they will look at the sunset and tremble.

In you, God knows, I've had the earthly life—
we were kind of religious, we thought in images.

As the final quotation suggests, the poet's personal life is an important part of the fabric. The poems to his wife and daughter include some of the most sensitive and the most wideranging philosophically. A self-characterization, of course, is the book's chief unity. It is a character more austere, less charming than the dreamer in Berryman's *Dream Songs*, perhaps the only recent work to which the *Notebook* can be compared.

In filling out the character, Lowell has reworked a number of poems from his earlier books, *Lord Weary's Castle, The Mills of the Kavanaughs, For the Union Dead*—formative experiences to which the journal-keeper seems to return naturally, as he reverts in new poems to events and persons we have already met. People from books and history and the arts appear and talk to us. Lowell is an intellectual *man* rather than an intellectual mind. History, literature, and art are among the things that have vividly befallen him in an eighteen-month period.

I suppose it is extravagant to speak of a book of poems as an act of propitiation. But when one of our best poets—only Pound, Auden, and Berryman can be named in the company now, I think—writes down all the patterns of his mind, he seems to be saying they are fragments of order. The poet—in all modesty, in all vanity—creates order, if at all, by arrangement. Where human response is as accurate as this, it becomes a hopeful kind of human sacrifice:

Reading Myself

Like millions, I took just pride and more than just,
first striking matches that brought my blood to boiling;
I memorized tricks to set the river on fire,
somehow never wrote something to go back to.
Even suppose I had finished with wax flowers
and earned a pass to the minor slopes of Parnassus . . .
No honeycomb is built without a bee
adding circle to circle, cell to cell,

the wax and honey of a mausoleum—
this round dome proves its maker is alive,
the corpse of such insect lives preserved in honey,
prays that the perishable work live long
enough for the sweet-tooth bear to desecrate—
this open book . . . my open coffin.

Henry Tasting All the Secret Bits of Life: Berryman's "Dream Songs"

The book John Berryman published last year is only his third, but it suggests that he is one of the best American poets writing today. *77 Dream Songs* is a fine and remarkable book of poems by any standards. It can be compared for delight, I think, to the best book of Wilbur or Roethke, to *Things of This World,* say, or *The Lost Son,* or even to *Lord Weary's Castle* though it is less perfect than Lowell's book, even of its raggeder kind. It can be compared for the account it gives of some of our troubles to *The Fire Next Time* or *Advertisements for Myself.* The latter comparisons are in Berryman's favor because he commits himself more generously than Baldwin or Mailer to a predicament he sees just as clearly. An example of this involvement can be seen in a Song about a week when the affairs of the Western World are going to hell with unusual deliberateness. Into this poem (66) Berryman interjects the following parenthesis of Eastern humility: "('All virtues enter into this world, but take one virtue, without which a man can hardly hold his own: that a man') Henry grew hot, got laid, felt bad, survived ('should always reproach himself.')."

It is a book of powerful originality, almost of eccentricity, and it presents difficulties at first. In the remarks that follow I will try to point out what I think are its chief distinctions and delights, and also to suggest what may stand, temporarily,

Wisconsin Studies in Contemporary Literature 6 (© 1965 by the Regents of the University of Wisconsin System); used by permission of the University of Wisconsin Press.

between these poems and a new reader. I will risk seeming to patronize the new reader rather than the poems, because after several careful readings of the book I am prepared to concede nothing. Berryman has long been famous as a poet's poet, with the contradiction that that forlorn phrase carries. This book should make him famous with everyone who uses modern poetry at all.

Two statements by the author about the "Dream Songs" are suggestive of how the poems are meant to be taken. Reading some of them in public two years ago he said, and has since allowed to be printed: "The poem is about a man who is apparently named Henry, or says he is. He has a tendency to talk about himself in the third person. His last name is in doubt. It's given at one point as Henry House and at other points as Henry Pussy-cat. He has a friend, moreover, who addresses him regularly as Mr. Bones, or some variation on that. Some of the sections . . . are really dialogues." In the present book he adds: "These are sections, constituting one version, of a poem in progress. . . . Many opinions and errors in the Songs are to be referred not to the character Henry, still less to the author, but to the title of the work."

In both cases the poet speaks of the poems as a single work, in spite of the fact that the eighteen-line Songs are often self-contained lyrics. And by calling attention to the dubious identity of "a man apparently named Henry" who entertains but is not accountable for "opinions and errors in the Songs," Berryman suggests that the unity of the work lies in its being the dream-autobiography of the central character. Whether this character calls himself *I* or *he*, Henry or Mr. Bones, his identity doesn't change. What does shift, with dream-like uncertainty, is the relationship of the dreamer to his dream self: am I acting this dream or watching it, or both? And who am I when I'm awake?

The discovery of Henry's whole identity, by him and by us, comprises the plot of the poem. It is a narrative poem and, as is true of a lot of literature, to discover its unity is to discover its meaning. A first reading of the poem will fasten on Songs that strike the individual reader as the most lucid and self-contained. He should not be put off by the ones that don't make any sense at first. (Some that began to shed light on and endear Henry to me were: Nos. 4, 7, 14, 18, 29, 35, 43, 62, 63, 69. Numbers in parentheses throughout refer to Songs rather than pages.)

Henry gradually emerges (to give the plot away) as a wholesome clean-cut American Proteus, a man with as many selves as our dreams confer. He commands the idiom, rhythm, and experience of a jazzman, both old-style New Orleans and hipster-junkie. He is equally at home with—or, more exactly, he can adapt himself with alcohol or Eastern philosophy to—a meeting of the Modern Language Association (35) and the role of Fulbright lecturer (out of season) on the Ganges (24, 71). He has read a lot more than I have and is more implicated in what he reads. He is generous, moral, and manic, but also lecherous, alcoholic, and depressive. Three songs treat directly with insanity (52–54) and half a dozen others touch on it familiarly. But through all the changes of his dreams the character and the voice remain so individual that you would no more mistake a song of Henry's, finally, than you would a meditation of Leopold Bloom's.

Henry's agonizing and beautiful energy is like that of Joyce's hero in another respect: it is profoundly, essentially humorous. The subconscious, which is chiefly what *Ulysses* and the "Dream Songs" record, knows no deliberate mode. It is not serious or joking, tragic or comic. It combines but doesn't rationally select, so that rational incongruity, a source of humor, is its habit:

> Two daiquiris
> withdrew into a corner of the gorgeous room
> and one told the other a lie.
>
> (16)

> That morning arrived to Henry as well a great cheque
> eaten out already by the Government & State &
> other strange matters . . .
>
> (19)

> Henry & Phoebe happy as cockroaches
> in the world-kitchen woofed . . .
>
> (31)

> Bats have no bankers and they do not drink
> and cannot be arrested and pay no tax
> and, in general, bats have it made.

(63)

Henry is an imaginary Negro (as the hero of Berryman's early short story is "The Imaginary Jew") and the poems draw on the several levels of humor that we owe to the Negro. Some of it runs deep and bitter, as it does in the blues, where only language and rhythm remain playful and even the word-play bites (40):

> I'm scared a lonely. Never see my son,
> easy be not to see anyone,
> combers out to sea
> know they're goin somewhere but not me.
> Got a little poison, got a little gun,
> I'm scared a lonely.
>
> I'm scared a only one thing, which is me,
> from othering I don't take nothin, see,
> for any hound dog's sake.
> But this is where I livin', where I rake
> my leaves and cop my promise, this' where we
> cry oursel's awake.
>
> Wishin was dyin but I gotta make
> it all this way to that bed on these feet
> where peoples said to meet.
> Maybe but even if I see my son
> forever never, get back on the take,
> free, black & forty-one.

Some of Henry's dreams are monologues and dialogues in the dialect of Negro vaudeville, a double-edged joke where the Negro plays it both cunning and obsequious, like an Elizabethan Fool, to amuse both himself and his slower-witted master. But Henry, being only an imaginary Negro, speaks mostly in a black-face parody of this, the vaudeville dialect of The Two Black Crows and Stepin Fetchit—a speech that has a rich, shrewd, rather brutal history in our national humor. Berryman refers once (72) to Henry's "burnt-cork luck." The phrase could be applied to the success with which this dialect gets at the truth in a world where the Negro's situation is both a symptom and a metaphor of our failure. The world is acutely perceived, in all its wonderful incomprehensibility, in this dialect:

> —Here matters hard to manage at de best,
> Mr. Bones. Tween what we see, what be,
> is blinds. Them blinds on fire.
>
> (64)

But against this perception is set the cliché of rational, white man's speech and the oversimplified, disastrous culture which that speech accommodates:

> There were strange gatherings. A vote would come
> that would be no vote. There would come a rope.
> Yes. There would come a rope.
> Men have their hats down. "Dancing in the Dark"
> will see him up, car-radio-wise. So many, some
> won't find a rut to park.
>
> It is in the administration of rhetoric,
> on these occasions, that—not the fathomless heart—
> the thinky death consists; . . .
>
> (10)

But these Negro masks are only one of Henry's identities. It would be more accurate to describe the hero of this poem as an imaginary madman. He identifies himself easily and completely with every sort of person and situation, even some that are totally unsympathetic. He has the inability of the insane to distinguish between things that are merely alike, and it is this that charges his metaphors with so much force. They are no longer implied comparisons but terrible uncertainties of identity. Song 48 is about Christ's wild cry to God from the cross (Mark 15) and about Henry's command of tourist phrases in foreign languages, and the two confuse in an image of the Eucharist:

> He yelled at me in Greek,
> my God!—It's not his language

and I'm no good at—his is Aramaic,
was—I am a monoglot of English
(American version) and, say pieces from
a baker's dozen others: where's the bread?

but rising in the Second Gospel, pal:
The seed goes down, god dies,
a rising happens,
some crust, and then occurs   an eating. He said so,
a Greek idea,
troublesome to imaginary Jews, . . .

In another (56) the dreamer changes abruptly into a deer, the completeness of the identification clinched by the term *two-footers* for men. Berryman's use of *tinchel* here, an obsolete Scots word meaning a ring formed by hunters to enclose deer, is unusual in its abstruseness but characteristic in its exactness:

The tinchel closes. Terror, & plunging, swipes.
I lay my ears back. I am about to die.
My cleft feet drum.
Fierce, the two-footers club. My green world pipes
a finish—for us all, my love, not some.

And often he holds to an insane accuracy of colloquial idiom and low image at moments when a sane man would be driven naturally to a more formal rhetoric:

I have been operating from *nothing,*
like a dog after its tail
more slowly, losing altitude.

(54)

Madman and black-face are real identities of the "man who is apparently named Henry," who is looking for wisdom and truth along with his identity. He insists on *wording* himself and his world exactly, as though the mystery might lie in words. (Of course it's self-conscious: he is a man who sleeps and wakes in an agony of self-consciousness—he's *our* man.) The poems seem to escape mannerism because Berryman never takes his eye off the scene, the event, the mood of Henry's dream. A grand style, or its parody, is frequently used:

> Our wounds to time, from all the other times,
> sea-times slow, the times of galaxies
> fleeing, the dwarfs' dead times,
> lessen so little that if here in his crude rimes
> Henry them mentions, do not hold it, please,
> for a putting of man down.
>
> (51)

As various as they are, we learn to recognize Henry's characteristic ways of wording himself and together they make a character. Style, Frost said, is the way a man takes himself.

The form of some of the poems is very strict. Song 42 is as exact a model of the stanza as I have found: pairs of iambic pentameter lines are followed by trimeter, and these are set in units of six lines and rhymed by various schemes. Some of the lines have very memorable and conventional rhythm:

> We dream of honor, and we get along.
>
> (42)

Against the strictly rhymed and scanned Songs are set some that are very free.

John Berryman's poems began appearing in magazines in the late 1930s. The first collection of them was in a New Directions volume in 1940 called *Five Young American Poets*. Six years later he published *The Dispossessed,* a book of lyrics that earned him the general regard of craftsmen in England as well as America. Among the *personae* offered by these poems are to be found recognizable fragments of the Dream Song hero and his patterns of speech. *The Dispossessed,* in fact, predicts *77 Dream Songs* more clearly than the brilliant narrative poem, *Homage to Mistress Bradstreet* that appeared in 1956. This is a strongly eccentric work whose difficulties are not as easily resolved as those of the "Dream Songs." Edmund Wilson said of it: "It seems to me the most distinguished long poem since *The Waste Land*." For many readers, it remains as inaccessible as Eliot's experiment, and they will not join Robert Lowell in placing it at the top of Berryman's accomplishments.

77 Dream Songs seems to me to deserve that rank. Moving forward with the intensity of vision that characterized *Mistress Bradstreet* and with the range of common experience of *The Dispossessed,* this work is free of the slight air of bookishness that hovered over Berryman's earlier work. (It is an air that hovers over all but the luckiest of modern poems.) The "Dream Songs" use a diction of their own, one that owes little to the familiar though flexible diction of current poetic practice. The language seems to spring naturally from the gusto (insane? holy?) with which Henry makes the human scene:

> Spry disappointments of men
> and vicing adorable children
> miserable women, Henry mastered, Henry
> tasting all the secret bits of life.

> (74)

Swan Songs

"For a while here we possessed an unusual man," he wrote in a song after Robert Frost's death in that earlier January. It is the kind of understatement you want to make about John Berryman, despairing of greater accuracy about such a poet and such a man, who wrote at the end

> O my Lord, I am not eloquent
> neither heretofore, nor since Thou hast spoken . . .
> but I am slow of speech, of a dim tongue.

Still, it is easier to review the last two books now. "Let too his giant faults appear, as sent together with his virtues down," he charged us in *Op. posth. no. 2.* Anybody who knew him knows that living he would have added, *posthumously, pal.*

What can be said now about the first two parts of *Love & Fame* is that they represent a difficult, deliberate artistic achievement: the foreswearing of the character (along with much of the strategy, the structure, and the sensibility) of the "Dream Songs"—the foreswearing of the accomplishment of twenty-five years, a major accomplishment of modern poetry. *77 Dream Songs,* which went to press in 1963, ends

> thése fierce & airy occupations, and love,
> raved away so many of Henry's years
> it is a wonder that, with in each hand
> one of his own mad books and all,
> ancient fires for eyes, his head full
> & his heart full, he's making ready to move on.

Poetry 122, no. 2 (May, 1973). Copyright © 1973 by The Modern Poetry Association. Reprinted by permission of the Editor of *Poetry.*

I don't think Berryman foresaw how long it was still to take to bring the "Dream Songs" to their conclusion—387 are now in print, counting the two apocryphal ones included in *Delusions, Etc.* But he was too good an artist, and too deeply versed in the metaphor of death and rebirth, not to recognize when an insight had come to its fulfillment.

In *Love & Fame* we discover him tearing up roots, going back to beginnings for a new start. The first part of the book is uneven or bad, but in the way the early work of a very original writer can be bad, through errors of taste or through pig-headedness or egotism. The poems are like those of a young writer trying to find out what his province is, more confident than he has any right to be that everything that happens to him is interesting, is in fact a poem.

Before he had written the "Eleven Addresses to the Lord," which constitute a tremendous breakthrough at the end of the book, he sent the earlier poems around to certain friends. Some of them must have said telling things. I think Mark Van Doren and Richard Wilbur are the two whose criticism he is quarreling with in *Message*.

> Amplitude,—voltage,—the one friend calls for one,
> the other for the other, in my work;
> in verse & prose. Well, hell.
> I am not writing an autobiography-in-verse, my friends.
>
> Impressions, structures, tales, from Columbia in the Thirties
> & the Michaelmas term at Cambridge in '36,
> followed by some later. It's not my life.
> That's occluded & lost.

The distinction was dear to him, like the distinction between the character of Henry, whose life paralleled his own so exactly, and his own. Neither distinction is clear to me.

Impressions, structures, tales. The unevenest poems are apt to yield vivid impressions like these:

> At the trial of the Earls
> ten years of venom flared forth in six words:
>
> when the great Ralegh rose to testify,
> Essex called out 'What boots it swear The Fox?'

Lacking the eighteen-line, mostly scanned and rhymed structure he had relied on almost exclusively for eight years and 4,000 lines, he settles now chiefly for a very loose four-line stanza. It is the freest verse of his career. Where there is organic form in the matter, there is form in the lyric, where not, not. Sometimes a scattered list of memories is pulled together conscientiously, mechanically, like this:

> Images, memories, of a lonely & ambitious young alien.
> Buildings, buildings & their spaces & decorations,
> are death-words & sayings in crisis.
> Old masters of old Cambridge, I am listening.

Another such ending, prosy but effective, is this:

> The thing meanwhile, I suppose, is to be courageous & kind.

The tales are successful almost in proportion as they are not autobiographical, especially as they are not sexually auto-biographical. Early in the book there is a poem starting:

> 'If I had said out passions as they were,'
> plain-saying Wordsworth confided deep down age,
> 'the poems could never have been published.'
> Ha! a confrère.

Wordsworth might demur at that brotherhood. These poems all *are* published, saying out passions as they were or even maybe touched up a little as most of us will when recounting tales of amatory prowess. The best tales in *Love & Fame* are in fact two compassionate but objective accounts of young women in a mental ward, "The Hell Poem" and "Death Ballad."

The book ends very strong. The "Addresses to the Lord" recount a religious conversion (an event that carries over into *Delusions, Etc.* both as plot and as craft). The verse becomes an easy iambic pentameter. The influence of Hopkins's syntax is more pronounced (to my ear: this is bound to be somewhat subjective) than anywhere else in Berryman. The poetry is superb.

Who am I worthless that You spent such pains
and take may pains again?
I do not understand; but I believe.
Jonquils respond with wit to the teasing breeze.

Induct me down my secrets. Stiffen this heart
to stand their horrifying cries, O cushion
the first the second shocks, will to a halt
in mid-air there demons who would be at me.

May fade before, sweet morning on sweet morning,
I wake my dreams, my fan-mail go astray,
and do me little goods I have not thought of,
ingenious & beneficial Father.

Ease in their passing my beloved friends,
all others too I have cared for in a travelling life,
anyone anywhere indeed. Lift up
sober toward truth a scared self-estimate.

Delusions, Etc. of John Berryman, as the title page of the book
reads, was seen through proofs by the poet and published last
April. The first nine poems, in much rougher quatrains than
the Addresses, have the titles of holy offices. The labor of
labored Hopkins sometimes is audible, and the poems are not
always even as graceful as these opening lines of "Matins."

> Thou hard. I will be blunt: Like widening
> blossoms again glad toward Your soothe of sun
> & solar drawing forth, I find meself
> little this bitter morning, Lord, tonight.
>
> Less were you tranquil to me in my dark
> just now than tyrannous.

But the emancipation from the "Dream Songs" is complete,
signalled perhaps by the inclusion of two old ones (published
before *Love & Fame* "in the [Harvard] *Advocate* devoted to my
Jazz") and by a stray line in another poem: "and as for Henry
Pussycat he'd just as soon be dead." There are at least four
major poems in the new-old unHenry'd voice that he seems to

have been rooting around for in the less successful parts of *Love & Fame*. A rangy voice it is. "Beethoven Triumphant" is a big poem, more than 120 lines. Robert Lowell calls it "the most ambitious and perhaps finest of his late poems, a monument to his long love, unhampered expression, and subtle criticism." It has the force and complexity of a late quartet or the Great Fugue.

The poem "In Memoriam" to Dylan Thomas is less objective, scaled down a little by autobiographical considerations but has a sureness of tone that the personal poems in *Love & Fame* did not generally achieve. "Scholars at the Orchid Pavilion" is one of his wittiest poems. Here are the first two stanzas:

Sozzled, Mo-tsu, after a silence, vouchsafed
a word alarming: 'We must love them all!'
Affronted, the fathers jumped.
'Yes' he went madly on and waved in quest
of his own dreadful subject 'O the fathers'
he cried 'must not be all!'
Whereat upon consent we broke up for the day.

The bamboo's bending power formed our theme
next dawn, under a splendid wind. The water
flapped to our tender gaze.
Girls came & crouched with tea. Great Wu pinched one,
forgetting his later nature. How the wind howled,
tranquil was our pavilion,
watching and reflecting, fingering bamboo.

"The Facts & Issues," the next-to-last poem in the book, is a tortuous self-examination. The tone is brutally colloquial for the religious context.

Let me be clear about this. It is plain to me
Christ underwent man & treachery & socks
& lashes, thirst, exhaustion, the bit, for my pathetic & disgust-
    ing vices,

to make this filthy fact of particular, long-after,
faraway, five-foot-ten & moribund
human being happy.

It's a hard poem. The experience in it is hard to take in, reconciling again two visions that tear the work (and the life) apart. ("These Songs are not meant to be understood, you understand. / They are only meant to terrify and comfort.")

There are at least two really happy poems in the book, "Minnesota Thanksgiving" and "Hello," the latter a welcome to his newest daughter, born the year before he died. There is evidence of a great deal of love and happiness in the life, the poems bear witness to that. But there are also two really terrible poems in *Delusions, Etc.,* one called "No" and this one:

He Resigns

Age, and the deaths, and the ghosts.
Her having gone away
in spirit from me. Hosts
of regrets come & find me empty.

I don't feel this will change.
I don't want any thing
or person, familiar or strange.
I don't think I will sing

any more just now;
or ever. I must start
to sit with a blind brow
above an empty heart.

This was a kind of resignation we had not expected, this final resigning *from,* by one who had so long managed just to resign himself *to,* the world. There had been so many wrestlings with the dark angel of suicide, and always at least to a respectful draw. "Anarchic Henry thought of laying hands / on Henry: haw! but the blood & the disgrace, / no, no, that's out" ("Dream Song 345"). "Now at last the effort to make him kill himself / failed" (359). And a line in *Love & Fame* (from "Purgatory"): "And if *you* can carry on *so,* so maybe can I."

Other quotations from this dear and masterly poet flood to our badly needed comfort now. "I hope that in my dying hour / nobody will be ashamed of me." (No. Proud, grateful, filled with wonder.) "Henry must desire / aplomb / at the temps / of the tomb." (He waved—"a final jauntiness in despair, an act of style," John Ciardi called it.) The last line of the last poem in this last book (Berryman as King David) reads: "all the black same I dance my blue head off!"

IV

Introductions and Addresses

Introduction to *Shelley's Poems*

The excellence of Shelley's best poems, which appears to advantage in a selection of this size, is hard to exaggerate. But for a hundred years after he died almost everything about him was exaggerated. His life, his death and his work were described in all the ways a protean century liked to see itself, and often they were drawn in flattering distortions which are not our style of flattery. Still, it is hard to know how to describe such people realistically; they themselves could not:

> We will each write a ghost story, said Lord Byron, and his proposition was eagerly acceded to. . . . On the morrow I announced that I had *thought of a story*. I began that day with the words, *It was on a dreary night of November*. . . . (Preface to *Frankenstein*, Mrs. Shelley.)

Mary Shelley was not quite nineteen that evening on the shore of Lake Leman, where they had recently journeyed so that her stepsister, sixteen, could continue an affair with Lord Byron, the oldest man in the room at twenty-eight. Shelley, who had fathered four children and lost one, would soon be twenty-four. He was perhaps the most unpredictable of the group:

> He once came upon me at Hampstead (Leigh Hunt wrote), when I had not seen him for some time; and after grasping my hands into both of his, in his usual fervent manner, he sat down, and looked at me very earnestly, with a deep, though

In *Shelley's Poems,* edited by William Meredith. Laurel Poetry Series. (Dell, 1962).

not melancholy interest in his face. We were sitting with our knees to the fire, to which we had been getting nearer and nearer, in the comfort of finding ourselves together. The pleasure of seeing him was my only feeling at the moment; and the air of domesticity about us was so complete, that I thought he was going to speak of some family matter, either his or my own, when he asked me, at the close of an intensity of pause, what was "the amount of the National Debt."

That summer in Switzerland, when Mary started *Frankenstein* (a task that was to hang over her until she was almost twenty), Shelley sometimes wrote after his signature in hotel ledgers, in Greek: *democrat, great lover of mankind, and atheist.* "Do you not think I shall do Shelley a service by scratching this out?" Byron said when he found one of these signatures, and did so.

But the self-characterization could not be effaced. It severely tried the honesty of his conventional admirers from the widowed Mary Shelley through Matthew Arnold. The reckless generosity of Shelley's mind led him to actions they could not approve and were tempted to misrepresent or suppress. After the French Revolution *democracy* meant something very like communism. As Shelley's life was lived, *great lover of mankind* brought to mind his repudiation of marriage. And if nineteenth-century gossip about Shelley and his women strikes us as malicious and uninformed, the *facts* of his amorous generosity toward himself and others simply do not lend themselves to conventional gossip. They lack, as a good many of Shelley's actions lacked, what the French critic has called *vraisemblance,* or likelihood. Neither women nor money seem to have meant to Shelley what they mean to most people, although they absorbed a great deal of his enormous energy.

Atheism was a more serious charge during Shelley's lifetime than today (he was expelled from Oxford for publishing an inquiry into religion) if only because religion was more central to social patterns. The free-thinking Godwin hurried to church to see Mary become an honest woman when Shelley was widowed. Shelley found it worth warning the inhabitants of Great Marlow (through an upholsterer) before he moved his family there in 1817 that they "would never go to church," and this must have contributed to the quiet they enjoyed there. "Ought we not to be happy?" Mary wrote from that place, where she finished *Frankenstein*, bore her first legitimate child, helped her stepsister take care of Byron's illegitimate daughter, and watched Shelley grow into a major poet as he wrote *The Revolt of Islam*. One can see, however, that Victorian critics would not have regarded her question as rhetorical.

Among a generation of remarkable eccentrics, Shelley holds his own very well, and perhaps it is that distortion of his character we have to resist today; it represents so small a part of him. Of distortions from the recent past, the figure of Shelley the sulky exquisite, waiting confidently for death and fame to deal with his bullies, seems the most warped. André Maurois drives the fair-minded reader to side with the businessmen, parents and educators who harassed Shelley, rather than with his impossible *Ariel*. Given more space, he might have made a sympathetic character of William Godwin. Of Shelley's schooldays Maurois wrote: "Only a few sensitive souls suffered terribly and suffered long." Current attempts to make Shelley *beat*, on the other hand, will have to deal with his good manners, his generosity and his studious and conscious artistry.

Of the distortions of the poems, the study of their philosophic content as an end in itself may well be the worst. We do not profitably subject Tennyson or Yeats to this kind of examination, although like Shelley they philosophized in rather unoriginal or unsophisticated ways; and what T. S. Eliot said of Shelley's ideas might better be said of Tennyson's or Yeats's: "he borrowed ideas—which, as I have said, is perfectly legitimate—but he borrowed shabby ones, and when he had got them he muddled them up with his own intuitions." I am afraid that we could describe the philosophic content of a great many fine lyric poems (though not, in all fairness, Mr. Eliot's) in these terms, and that they show a false premise. The discoveries of a lyric poet which chiefly interest us are those concerning language and imagery. Shelley's discoveries about certain verbal effects—sounds and ideas and feelings which exist once only, incarnate in certain dispositions of English words—these are often what his poems are *about,* as is the case, it seems to me, with much great lyric poetry. What we learn from poetry is not so much the *nature* of experience as the *force* of it.

A recent neglect of Shelley has allowed the legend to quiet down, restoring the man to a vast and elliptic body of facts, and the poems to our fresh attention as mere poems. In Newman Ivey White's two-volume *Shelley* and in letters and memoirs there emerges a mind that is irresistibly energetic and curious. But good poems do not depend on biography, and none have been included here for their biographical interest. Shelley's poetry has gained from the fact that no one *has* to read it any more, let alone its century-long accumulation of largely biographical criticism. Whoever likes poetry will find here the musical and figurative virtuosity that interested Browning, Arnold, and Yeats, and led Wordsworth (whom Shelley had attacked) to say in 1827: "Shelley is one of the best *artists* of us all: I mean in workmanship of style." In the rest of this appreciation I will speak of Shelley's *numbers,* as Wordsworth called a poet's music, and of his imagery.

Shelley's ear for poetry was very sensitive, but it was also a little willful or eccentric. He seems to have felt that the power of rhyme—a magic property of words, capable of heroic feats of association—was sufficient to put down all the enemies of rhyme: chiefly inaccuracy of statement and idiom, but also clichés of sound and sense. Yet it was this predilection for rhyme, and for very strong, almost singsong rhythms, that accomplished his greatest effects. The restless urgency of "Ode to the West Wind" is partly the result of the way the lines drive *through* some of Shelley's strongest and most conventional triple rhymes, as when we come (past *towers* and *flowers*) to these lines:

> Thou
> For whose path the Atlantic's level powers
>
> Cleave themselves into chasms, while far below
> The sea-blooms and the oozy woods which wear
> The sapless foliage of the ocean, know

Thy voice, and suddenly grow gray with fear,
And tremble and despoil themselves: oh, hear!

The terrible force of "Similes for Two Political Characters of 1819" is driven home by its rhymes, and especially by the insistent polysyllabic rhymes, *clarion-carrion* and *battle-rattle-cattle.*

I

As from an ancestral oak
    Two empty ravens sound their clarion,
Yell by yell, and croak by croak,
When they scent the noonday smoke
    Of fresh human carrion:—

II

As two gibbering night-birds flit
    From their bowers of deadly yew
Through the night to frighten it,
When the moon is in a fit,
    And the stars are none, or few:—

III

As a shark and dog-fish wait
    Under an Atlantic isle,
For the negro-ship, whose freight
Is the theme of their debate,
    Wrinkling their red gills the while—

IV

Are ye, two vultures sick for battle,
    Two scorpions under one wet stone,
Two bloodless wolves whose dry throats rattle,
Two crows perched on the murrained cattle,
    Two vipers tangled into one.

The four-beat line of this poem is the same powerful, rhythmic seven-syllable line that makes memorable such various works as William Browne's "On the Dowager Countess of Pembroke" (*Underneath this sable hearse / Lies the subject of all verse*), Blake's "The Tiger" (*Tiger! Tiger! burning bright / In the forests of the night*), Yeats's "Under Ben Bulben" (*Irish poets, learn your trade, / Sing whatever is well made*), and Auden's "In Memory of W. B. Yeats" (*Earth, receive an honored guest; / William Yeats is laid to rest*). The strictness of the line, in all the uses cited, gives a sense of powerful emotion contained by powerful decorum, although in Shelley's poem the decorum is ironic. The effect is much less securely achieved in his fragment called "Death."

I

Death is here and death is there,
Death is busy everywhere,
All around, within, beneath,
Above is death—and we are death.

II

Death has set his mark and seal
On all we are and all we feel,
On all we know and all we fear,
. . . .

III

First our pleasures die—and then
Our hopes, and then our fears—and when
These are dead, the debt is due,
Dust claims dust—and we die too.

IV

All things that we love and cherish,
Like ourselves must fade and perish;
Such is our rude mortal lot—
Love itself would, did they not.

The weakness of this poem is not, I think, what Cleanth Brooks and Robert Penn Warren suggest in *Understanding Poetry*, that "the specific feeling stimulated by the jigging rhythm tends to contradict the response suggested by the ideas, images, etc. of the poem." The poem fails because Shelley, knowing that this rhythm is capable of containing strong feeling, has trusted the rhythm too far, has in fact asked it to carry the slack weight of some very trivial diction and banal rhymes. I doubt that a specific feeling is generated by *any* rhythm, but the poems by William Browne and Auden above demonstrate that this rhythm is not incapable of solemn effects. The fragment (which *is* a fragment, let it be insisted in Shelley's defense) seems to ask more of the tense seven-syllable line than a line alone can carry; but as for "jigging," it jigs like a perfectly good gallows song.*

Shelley's use of traditional versification is skillful and carefully acquired. The household at Great Marlow read Spenser in the evening when he was writing *The Revolt of Islam,* a work in Spenserian stanzas almost as long as the present selection of his poems. In the same year he started a long poem, *Prince Athanase,* in *terza rima,* which is the verse form of his last major poem. His use of *ottava rima* in *The Witch of Atlas* is as distinctive as Yeats's use of it or Byron's. (The bantering tone of the dedicatory stanzas of "his Witch" to Mary reminds us how intimately he was associated with *Don Juan.*) At a period when Pope was considered a tyrant of verse, Shelley wrote thousands of couplets. He made these forms his own and treated some of them, the sonnet in particular, very freely.

This patience with established verse forms, in a genius otherwise impatient of everything established, suggests that Shelley was unusually responsive to the expressive power of forms themselves. Possibly this is what Wordsworth's puzzling phrase, "workmanship of style," meant to point out. Such workmanship places Shelley in the tradition of Tennyson, Poe, and Swinburne, poets whose "music" is bought at some cost to the other elements of poetry but also accounts for their most complete successes. The failures of these poets are like certain failures of Shelley, when the costume of a poem seems to come to the banquet with nobody inside it. Six discarded lines make this point with breathtaking brevity. (We should not blame Shelley

---

*When T. S. Eliot attacks what he calls a *jingling* passage from *Prometheus Unbound,* he is right to say it jingles. Shelley's ear contains full orchestration. I agree with Mr. Eliot that to beat a triangle solo at that point was unmusical. (Both of Mr. Eliot's criticisms mentioned here are from the essay cited in the bibliography [of *Shelley's Poems*], which records an honest and intelligent prejudice.)

for snippets his widow and others have printed which he had put aside.)

To Mary Shelley

The world is dreary,
And I am weary
Of wandering on without thee, Mary;
A joy was erewhile
In thy voice and thy smile
And 'tis gone, when I should be gone too, Mary.

Shelley's poems are as remarkable for their images as for their music. Throughout them we encounter objects, animals, and human figures which have an ambience of their own, an unspecific reference to a rich, mysterious world of their own. Shelley had a peculiar sense of the independent existence of an image, of its quality (which W. H. Auden and Norman Holmes Pearson have said turns an image into a symbol) of being "charged with more affect than a rational inspection can account for." Where his images become symbols, they carry their own meanings and we do not need a reader's guide.

In most poems, it does not occur to us to ask what Shelley or his subconscious *meant* by the images. If they are ambiguous, they are so only as the world itself declines to give us yes or no. The poet does not solve mysteries that have been riddled into the universe, but "strips the veil of familiarity from the world, and lays bare the naked and sleeping beauty, which is the spirit of its forms." "The spirit of its forms" is mysterious, and an image must not be shorn of its strangeness.

"A Defense of Poetry" has other things to say about the shadowy world of imagery. "[The Poet's] language is vitally metaphorical; that is, it marks the before unapprehended relations of things"; and: "A poem is the very image of life expressed in its eternal truth. There is this difference between a story and a poem, that a story is a catalogue of detached facts *which have no other connection than time, place, circumstance, cause and effect.*"

These connections are, of course, all the rational connections. A poem doesn't violate them deliberately (or didn't use to) but rather is unconcerned with them. As an example of how rich and ambiguous, and still how self-explanatory, Shelley's images can be, here is a fragment from the year 1819 which "makes familiar objects be as if they were not familiar." The image of the serpent is used in three of Shelley's long poems and had acquired for him, and ideally for the reader, associations of a specific kind. But simply as an image, in this fragment the serpent has the reality or hyper-reality of Emily Dickinson's "A narrow fellow in the grass"; it is "charged with more affect than a rational inspection can account for."

> Wake the serpent not—lest he
> Should not know the way to go,—
> Let him crawl which yet lies sleeping
> Through the deep grass of the meadow!
> Not a bee shall hear him creeping,
> Not a may-fly shall awaken
> From its cradling blue-bell shaken,
> Not the starlight as he's sliding
> Through the grass with silent gliding.

"Poetry is ever accompanied with pleasure," Shelley said in "A Defense of Poetry." There are a number of other statements in that excited essay to show that he thought of poetry more joyfully than many readers and critics have assumed. If it is a mistake to think of Shelley as a self-pitying man, it is a worse one to think of his poems as melancholy. They were apparently an unremitting source of pleasure to him, which even their chilling unacceptance could scarcely dim. "The joy of the perception and still more of the creation of poetry, is often wholly unalloyed," he wrote in the "Defense" a year before his death. Even in the most pessimistic works (and I agree with Harold Bloom that the last major poem, *The Triumph of Life*, is also the most somber) there is, in Yeats's phrase, a "gaiety transfiguring all that dread." Art by its very nature asserts at least two kinds of good—order and delight. In Shelley's words again, "Sorrow, terror, anguish, despair itself are often the chosen expressions of an approximation of the highest good."

The poems in this selection were chosen to give delight. They were written by a voluble young man of genius between his twenty-second year and his death at just under thirty, and they represent only a fraction of his work. But they carry his pleasure in language and vision. The earliest one contains these lines:

> The cloud shadows of midnight possess their own repose,
>   For the weary winds are silent, or the moon is in the deep:
> Some respite to its turbulence unresting ocean knows;
>   Whatever moves, or toils, or grieves, hath its appointed
>   sleep.

The latest one opens:

> Swift as a spirit hastening to his task
> Of glory and of good, the Sun sprang forth . . .

The lyric exuberance of these lines, and of the whole brief career lying between them which this book tries to represent, is hard to resist. Shelley's powers increase so regularly that to project them only a few more years—say to the age of thirty-six, when Byron died—suggests a poet greater than any the nineteenth century produced in English. Keats, of course, suggests as much and more.

We must try to be grateful for what we have, and that can be done partly by accuracy. It is not likely that another reputable scholar will ever say, as Newman Ivey White did in 1940, "Shelley is now generally recognized as one of the four or five greatest English poets since Shakespeare." But it is not likely either that poets as perceptive as Allen Tate and T. S. Eliot will again feel the need to minimize him as they did once, when his exaggerated reputation had still to be brought into line with a "new" poetry. In the end good poetry tends to be compatible with all other good poetry. I will not hazard Shelley's fortunes again with unsubstantiated claims, but prefer to dare anyone who thinks him an overrated poet to look within.

Invitation to Miss Elizabeth Bishop

With an Epigraph and Invocation and Fourteen Maxims

The Epigraph

I chose her because she's my favorite living poet.
—*John Ashbery, nominating Miss Bishop for the Books*
Abroad—Neustadt International Prize for Literature

The Invocation

From 437 Lewis Wharf, by Amtrak's uncertain rails
    trailing your zip-code one four two two six,
come dawdling down from Boston this late December day
    crossing the Harlem River thin as Styx
to where Session 565 lovingly travails,
    claiming your vast geographies for MLA.
Come dawdling anyway.

The Maxims

1. We speak of certain artists as great, others as important, still others, grudgingly, as original. When we say, *I choose her because she's my favorite poet,* we praise a one-to-one relationship with a writer who alters our lives a little for the better.

In *Elizabeth Bishop and Her Art,* edited by Lloyd Schwartz and Sybil P. Estess (University of Michigan Press, 1983). Originally delivered at the Modern Language Association Convention, 1976.

2. The scholars of literature and the makers of it are said to exist in a symbiotic relationship. But at best the relationship is more comradely than that: we have both bet our sweet lives on the efficacy of literature to alter human lives a little for the better. (That famous elegy which tells us that poetry makes nothing happen, ends, you will recall, by asking the dead poet to alter our lives vastly for the better.)

3. When Elizabeth Bishop published her *Complete Poems*—eighty-five of them, counting five translations she laid especial claim to—we realized that we had grown sadly accustomed to *incomplete* ones.

4. The *oeuvre* is small, like Piero della Francesca's and Sappho's, but here elimination has been achieved by a more deliberate process than time and accidental loss.

5. One wonders whether, if poet X had published only Miss Bishop's now total of eighty-five poems instead of his seventeen books, two *Selecteds* and one medium-sized and one mammoth *Collected Poems,* a silky confection of sows' ears might have resulted. One thinks that unlikely. The stuff is different.

6. A sign of major vision: the artist is as careful to bring the small insight to perfection as the large. "Late Air" is no less a Bishop poem, no more a Bishop poem than "Visits to St. Elizabeths."

7. Foolish critics "judge a problem by its awkwardness," in Auden's phrase, measure a poem by its pretension, as if David had never picked up a slingshot or Emily Dickinson a robin.

8. Foolish critics reproached Frost and Auden—very early on, it now appears—for little poems, small themes, taking these for trivia, signs of decline in powers. Miss Bishop was too quick for them. From the first, she has cut small jewels along with the large.

9. The appropriateness of form in these poems constitutes a lucid, enduring maxim which only a very unwise person would try to paraphrase. I would paraphrase it, *total attention.*

10. We are accustomed to a certain technical sloppiness in revolutionary artists. We used to speak tolerantly of the nurse-maid who "threw out the baby with the bath water," although nobody really approved of that. What are we to say of the nurseries today, with the window wide open, dirty bath water steaming in the basin, and no baby to be found?

11. If you want to see perfection of organic form, look at "Visits to St. Elizabeths" (a round), "Sandpiper" (quatrains), the "Sestina" ("September rain falls on the house. . . ."), "One Art" (a villanelle) and "Roosters" (triplets). Clean babies.

12. She will yet civilize and beguile us from our silly schools. The Olsons will lie down with the Wilburs and the Diane Wakoskis dance quadrilles with the J. V. Cunninghams and the Tooth Mother will suckle the rhymed skunk kittens of Lowell.

13. The two kinds of poetry are, Excellent and Other (as with scholarship). They cannot lie down together because somebody always gets squashed.

14. Elizabeth Bishop, so far as we know, writes only the one kind. Most other poets show off, in print, their greater versatility.

Foreword to *Robert Frost Country*

Theodore Morrison, whose friendship with Robert Frost started earlier than my own, has made the point that Frost is not a nature poet, in the Wordsworthian sense of the term, "but rather a poet who is also a countryman, who knows his birds and botany, his woods and farms and all their uses, too well to be fooled." I think Frost would have felt that many of the Melvins' pictures take the same knowing look: they see New England as the habitation of particular flora and fauna, with a predominant interest in the fauna called New Englanders, and their spoor.

Looking at the handsome account of Frost's country in these pages, one is struck by how completely the visual and the verbal experiences differ. The moment of revelation which the poet attends on is different from the photographer's, and the means by which he fixes it are different. Some effects, some visual images, may allow for literal translation of feeling, but most comparisons between pictures and poems can only hope to establish some sort of equivalence. I can't speak with a craftsman's authority about these photographs, and they don't need that. But some of Frost's verbal effects dramatize the difference between the two arts.

In "Hyla Brook," for instance, he speaks of the spring peepers, "That shouted in the mist a month ago / Like ghost of sleigh-bells in a ghost of snow." That is perhaps as much physical experience as can be compressed into twenty syllables, yet it works directly neither on our visual nor our auditory imagination, but rather exists as an astonishing verbal experience. The playfulness of the image of ghosts is word-playfulness, which we translate only later into the aural and visual experiences. Peepers *do* sound like sleigh-bells (not everybody remembers the high, shrill dissonance of sleigh-bells), and early spring mist *can* impersonate the other vague white element it has lately supplanted. Our senses work like that, when surprised. But it is the sheer compression of those eighteen words, their focusing of the lens of simile, that makes the poem lodge itself in our verbal imagination. "The utmost of ambition is to lodge a few poems where they will be hard to get rid of," he wrote. "Hyla Brook" ends with the line, "We love the things we love for what they are." What poems *are*, of course, is an astonishment of words.

Frost's famous puns could be likened to the photographer's technique of double exposure. (Both devices require some sophistication, to make an insight out of a confusion.) In "The Ax-Helve," when the French-Canadian craftsman has finished carving the helve and mounted the axhead, "he brushed the shavings from his knee / And stood the ax there on its horse's hoof, / Erect, but not without its waves, as when / The snake stood up for evil in the Garden—"

Here the exposure (in the photographer's sense) is triple: there's the double meaning of *stood up for,* but there is also the echo of Milton's Latinism in *not without* and *as when,* which makes of the lines a playful incursion into what remains, for most of us, Milton's park. It is a scene Frost will pun on again in later years in a poem called "Away!", the only poem that treats directly on his own death:

> Don't think I leave
> For the outer dark
> Like Adam and Eve
> Put out of the Park.
>
> Forget the myth.
> There is no one I
> Am put out with
> Or put out by.

Then there is the texture of light you hear photographers talk about, which I believe has an equivalent in the poet's texture of sound. The poet sets his ear for a given scene the way a photographer sets his lens. Frost's poem " 'Out, out—' " tells of a boy whose hand is cut off by a saw-blade, and who dies as much from the realization as for any medical reason:

> The boy's first outcry was a rueful laugh,
> As he swung toward them holding up his hand,
> Half in appeal, but half as if to keep
> The life from spilling. Then the boy saw all—
>
> He saw all spoiled.

He saw all spoiled. The four words are *lighted* with a terrible light. Slow, accented syllables (*spondaic,* the prosodist calls them), they act out the grief with a bleak, drawn-out, voweled sound which it is not excessive to compare with Lear's heartbroken cry over the dead Cordelia. "Thou'lt come no more."

Frost had a wonderful ear for the way people declare themselves in speech—variously, and so as to identify both their character and some immediate dramatic response. He listened for these "sounds of sense" (as he called them) as much as to the data they overlay. He occasionally said, as his hearing dimmed in his later years, that he'd rather be blind than deaf. I think he meant by that only that his ears astonished him more than his eyes did. But his eyes were lesser only as a giant's toes may be shorter and less prehensile than his fingers. He looked with the same fierce attention that he listened with.

Once when I was driving him home from a visit to my college, I stopped for gas on the Connecticut Turnpike. Between the gasoline pumps hung large metal cylinders, perhaps three feet long and a foot in diameter, which I had not until then ever seen, though they'd been there since the turnpike opened. Frost asked me what they were. He kept hoping that my years as an aviator had made me attentive to mechanical things. But I had learned, the hard way, not to fake answers to him. So he asked the attendant, wiping his side of the windshield.

"They're for quick oil changes," the boy said. "You put one hose under the crankcase and the other in the top, and you can change oil as quick as you can fill a gas tank."

"Do you use them much?" Frost asked.

"Nope," the boy said.

"Why not?" He was interested.

"They don't work."

"Never did work?"

"Never did work."

Frost shared his pleasure at this successful exposure with me, but all the way to Cambridge I was looking at things with the attention of a madman, to see what else I hadn't seen. He was eighty-five, I was a dim-sighted forty, but in the kingdom of the dim-sighted, the man who pays attention is king.

I expect the Melvins would feel as diffident as I am (*scared* was the word I would have used when he walked the earth, though I loved him) to say what Frost would have made of these pictures; but I know he admired acts of attention.

Foreword to *The Collected Prose of Robert Hayden*

Robert Hayden was a man as gifted in humanity as he was in poetry. His death in Ann Arbor, Michigan, on February 25, 1980, struck a host of readers like a personal loss, and acquaintances felt it like friends. The several memorials I went to seemed as intimate as wakes—it was as though there were no ranks of friendship among those who had known him, no degrees of loss.

There can be no ranks either among those who want his work to be more widely known and more generally available. In assembling this collection of his prose, Frederick Glaysher has done something that all friends of Hayden's achievement must be grateful for. These works comprise a lovely and enduring miscellany which the poet himself might have been too reticent to put forth as a book. But they belong in company with the too-small, imperishable body of his poems. In their different ways, each of them is open and generous-minded like their author.

He was born in the poor section of Detroit called Paradise Valley, in 1913. The ironical name of this slum area may have provided one of his earliest insights into the wry poetry of his people. In any case, he invoked it near the end of his life in the title and subjects of a fine autobiographical sequence in *American Journal.* He went to public schools in Detroit and, as we read in "Some Remembrances" here, won a scholarship to

---

In *The Collected Prose of Robert Hayden,* edited by Frederick Glaysher (University of Michigan Press, 1984).

Detroit City College. He went on to do graduate work at the University of Michigan, where he came to know W. H. Auden—he says he "studied with" him, but that's not the term Auden used about a poet for whom he came to have a high regard. Both poets were to die too soon, at sixty-seven. Hayden published his first book at twenty-seven, in 1940.

After graduate school, he went to Nashville and taught for more than two decades at Fisk University. His final teaching years were at the University of Michigan. He left Ann Arbor for other posts twice, once to teach at Connecticut College for a semester, and again in 1976–78 to serve as Consultant in Poetry to the Library of Congress.

A man of natural dignity, Robert Hayden accepted the many honors that came to him in later years modestly, as he had accepted neglect for most of his life philosophically. Besides the Poetry Consultancy, these honors were to include the Grand Prize for Poetry at the First World Festival of Negro Arts in Dakar in 1976, the Fellowship of the Academy of American Poets, the Loines Award (first given to Robert Frost), and later membership in the American Academy and Institute of Arts and Letters, several honorary degrees, and an invitation to read at the Carter White House. Coming after years of remarkable writing and teaching this recognition gratified but did not perceptibly change him from the gentle, powerful, original, and solitary genius he had always been.

In the 1960s, Hayden declared himself, at considerable cost in popularity, an American poet rather than a black poet, when for a time there was posited an unreconcilable difference between the two roles. There is scarcely a line of his which is not identifiable as an experience of black America, but he would not relinquish the title of American writer for any narrower identity.

When he was in Providence in 1976 to receive an honorary degree from Brown University he told of an experience at Ann Arbor when he first went back there to teach. A young black man came to his office one day, not on literary business but to reproach him for his dress. "How can you, a black man, come to your office day after day wearing a suit like that, the uniform of your white oppressor?" Hayden was elegantly dressed that morning in Providence, when he told the story. "I've always liked to dress myself up a little," he said then, "and I told this boy, 'I'm just coming into my style, boy. You ain't seen nothin' yet.'"

It was his work to share and enlighten the American black experience, not to diminish it by rancor. This he did by the difficult, simple method of almost flawless art, an art which finally called so loud across the chasm of race that, at last, he was heard on both sides, reminding us of our humanity. His is a complex vision of mutual responsibility. He maintained it optimistically, as he maintained his Baha'i faith and his high personal code. In a famous poem called "The Whipping" he found an emblem for his compassion. The poem begins by appealing to our sense of terrible injustice, as we watch an old woman pursue and beat a young boy with uncontrollable rage. Then the woman's rage and ours subside as the speaker tells of whippings of his own childhood, "the blows, the fear worse than blows that hateful words could bring, the face that I no longer knew or loved." And then, miraculously, the poem melts with truth:

> Well, it is over now, it is over,
>   and the boy sobs in his room,
>
> And the woman leans muttering against
>   a tree, exhausted, purged—
> avenged in part for lifelong hidings
>   she has had to bear.

I think it is this remarkable capacity for compassion which kept him from joining causes where anger took precedence over understanding. He understood but was committed to contend with Auden's dire pronouncement: "Those to whom evil is done / do evil in return," and his life and his work were attempts to break that cycle.

Memorial for René Dubos

(In keeping with the conservative policies of our organization, which waited until René Dubos was in his late seventies to elect him to our body, I have waited fourteen months after his death to read this memorial. Although I believe I was his proposer, what I have learned from reading his life and work during the past year have made me marvel more than ever that such a humane and civilized Gallic giant moved among us. In his second or probably third language—he lived in Italy when he was twenty-one to twenty-three—he was not, I think, a great American stylist. His literacy was that of a scientist turned prophet, and one would no more rap his knuckles for a certain stiffness of style than quarrel with Whitman or Dreiser about reticence. That we had the wit to elect him shows us on the whole to be the superior judges we lay claim in our elections to be. These remarks are not part of the memorial but a personal expression of honor at having been asked to write it.)

René Dubos was born in 1901 in the small French city of Saint Brice-sous-Foret and grew up in the small agricultural villages of the Ile-de-France north of Paris. His father's death from a head wound suffered in the Great War necessitated his giving up a career as a scholar of history. He entered the Institut National Agronomique and took a B.S. degree. For two years he edited a scientific journal in Rome and then in 1924 came to the United States, where he spent the rest of his life.

Address delivered to the American Academy Institute of Arts and Letters, 1983.

It was a life in which he identified certain critical encounters. At the age of ten he contracted rheumatic fever and over the next seven years, while restricted in physical activity, he cultivated a habit of meditating Hippolyte Taine's "Essay on the Fables of La Fontaine," which he read at the age of fifteen, and which had a lasting effect on him. Taine's thesis that the spirit of the fables can be accounted for by the landscape where the author lived made Dubos aware of the influence of environment on an individual's development, a theory which became a mystique for him as a scientist. In Rome, in 1932 he read in a French journal a semi-popular science article by a Russian bacteriologist named Sergei Winogradsky which contended that soil microbes should be studied in their own environment, not in pure cultures grown in laboratories. The idea that microbes might have a different life history under natural rather than artificial conditions struck him so forcibly that he decided to become a bacteriologist. "This is really where my scholarly life began," he said later. "I have been restating that idea in all forms ever since."

By the kind of happy accident that became his special response to the world, he guided around Rome to earn money for his passage to America. A Rutgers microbiologist who would later become a Nobel laureate met him on the ship carrying them to America, and he took his Ph.D. at Rutgers under this scientist, Selman Wakesmam.

Another influence was Louis Pasteur, about whom Dubos wrote two books, and from whom he said he got the idea which enabled him to find the enzyme which would break down the protective capsule protecting the bacteria causing lobar pneumonia. It had been Pasteur who maintained that in some form or another natural energy exists to break down or decompose any organic substance. The scientist Oswald T. Avery, who predicted DNA in 1944, was influential in calling Dubos to the Rockefeller Institute in 1927 (now Rockefeller University), where he remained as Emeritus Professor, except for two years at Harvard, until his death. His experimental work laid grounds for the practical use of antibiotics, and he was a pioneer in this field.

His last and probably most enduring scientific discovery

has to do with what he learned from Hippolyte Taine. He argued that the greatest threat to humankind may not be the environmental hazards we are creating but our capacity to adapt to them—an accommodation which can occur only by means of disastrous social and cultural mechanisms. "It is not man the ecological crisis threatens to destroy," he wrote in 1970, "but the quality of human life, the attributes that make human life different from animal life . . . What we call humanness is the expression of the interplay between man's nature and the environment, an interplay which is as old as life itself and which is the mechanism for creation on earth." His language in that article for the old *Life* magazine is characteristically straight and unembellished and conventional, as though he had foresworn style for some greater urgency. He was fired with prophetic zeal in his last books. Less humor lightens their message, but there is a compensating beauty of precision. Anyone can read them, and he knew the problems of readership in his adopted and beloved country.

"The most deplorable aspect of existence in American cities," he wrote, "may not be murder, rape and robbery, but the constant exposure of children to pollutants, noise, ugliness and garbage in the streets. This constant exposure conditions children to accept public squalor as the normal state of affairs and thereby handicaps them mentally at the beginning of their lives."

His writing after 1960 was more and more concerned with the science of ecology. In 1969 his book *So Human an Animal: How We Are Shaped by Surroundings and Events* shared a Pulitzer Prize in nonfiction with Norman Mailer. In 1972 he and Barbara Ward published a book which remains, the *New York Times* said in his obituary, a fundamental work in the field, *Only One Earth*, a work commissioned by the Secretary General of the United Nations Conference on the Human Environment.

In a late interview, he spoke on genetics. "I admit that, yes, we know fairly well the mechanisms by which hereditary characteristics are transferred—but from there to state that we understand *life!* This is a word which, as we use it, is simply not encompassed by a molecule. Life implies an organization, an ability to change, even a 'capacity to blunder' as Lewis

Thomas cleverly points out in *The Medusa and the Snail*. . . . There's a great mystery in this phenomenon we call life."

He was a tangible presence at our meetings. A tall, grave, deep-voiced, humorous man, he spoke only generously, and he spoke as a populist, in plain if formal language. His great heart stopped on his eighty-first birthday, February 20, 1982.

The last words I remember hearing from him, by the way—he and I had proposed Lewis Thomas for membership in 1980—were these: "What should we do next about getting Lew Thomas in here?"

In Praise of Instinct

The instinct that I want to praise is the troublesome human impulse to love one another impractically, socially, brother and sisterly. The reason it seems appropriate for me to talk about it in chapel is that I find in this instinct a kind of argument from design: there appears to me to be, for each man and woman, a created identity to be found in his own working out of this mode of relationship. By learning how we belong to one another, we learn who we are, no two alike.

A society can make this discovery very difficult for some or all of its members. I think of Wilfred Owen. A Company Commander in the First World War, he was awarded the Military Cross for exceptional bravery in the field before he was killed at twenty-five. Toward the end of his brief life he wrote a version of the Abraham and Isaac story which we have just heard. He seems to have had an instinct for sacrifice—that is what bravery meant in the citations of that war—and an instinct for peace, and he fulfilled both of these drives to love his fellow man, the one by his death, the other by his poems. This poem is called "The Parable of the Old Man and the Young."

> So Abram rose, and clave the wood, and went,
> And took the fire with him, and a knife.
> And as they sojourned both of them together,
> Isaac the first-born spake and said, My Father,
> Behold the preparations, fire and iron,

Address delivered at Harkness Chapel, Connecticut College, September, 1972.

But where the lamb for this burnt-offering?
Then Abram bound the youth with belts and straps,
And builded parapets and trenches there,
And stretched forth the knife to slay his son.
When lo! an angel called him out of heaven,
Saying, Lay not thy hand upon the lad,
Neither do anything to him. Behold,
A ram, caught in a thicket by its horns;
Offer the Ram of Pride instead of him.
But the old man would not so, but slew his son,
And half the seed of Europe, one by one.

Another statement about how hard we make the finding of this lover's role is in Dostoyevsky's "The Dream of a Ridiculous Man." The narrator is telling of a dream he had about how men fell from the perfect love which their instinct had once made natural. He says, "There arose men who began to think how to bring all people together again, so that everybody, while still loving himself best of all, might not interfere with others, and all might live together in something like a harmonious society. Regular wars sprang up over this idea."

What Owen attributed to the Great War (as for twenty years we naively called it, thinking it was the last one), and what Dostoyevsky attributed to self-love on a general scale, Kurt Vonnegut has recently blamed on simply the size of our society, saying that we evolved as an animal chemically equipped for tribal life in small units, and are incapable of tribal brotherhood on the scale we are forced to engage one another today. He recalls an old teacher of his from whom he learned this—and he quotes him:

In a folk society, says Dr. Redfield . . . "behavior is personal, not impersonal. A 'person' may be defined as that social object which I feel to respond to situations as I do, with all the sentiments and interests which I feel to be my own; a person is myself in another form, his qualities and values are inherent within him, and his significance for me is not merely one of utility. A 'thing,' on the other hand, is a social object which has no claim upon my sympathies, which responds to me, as I conceive it, mechanically; its value for me exists insofar as it serves my end. In the folk society, all human beings admitted to the society are treated as persons; one does not deal impersonally ('thing fashion') with any other participant in the little world of that society." "And I say to you," Vonnegut goes on, "that we are full of chemicals that require us to belong to folk societies, or, failing that, to feel lousy all the time. We are chemically engineered to live in folk societies, just as fish are chemically engineered to live in clean water. . . ."

Chemicals make us furious when we are treated as things rather than persons. When anything happens to us which would not happen in a folk society, our chemicals make us feel like fish out of water. Our chemicals demand that we get back into water again. If we become increasingly wild and preposterous in modern times—well, so do fish on riverbanks, for a little while.

If we become increasingly apathetic in modern times,— well, so do fish on river banks, after a little while. Our children often come to resemble apathetic fish—except that fish can't play guitars. And what do many of our children attempt to do? They attempt to form folk societies, which they call "Communes." Wars, greed, impersonality: no one can deny that these forces make the response of brotherhood difficult, though the more history one has, I suspect, the less sure one is that we have increased the jeopardy to love. It has always been a perilous quest, men and women have always had to bet their sweet lives on it. Many of our soundest instincts are reckless, the religious one perhaps most of all.

The instinct of the artist seems to me one of reckless generosity. We let our artists look in the chasm for us and come back and tell us what they see: we can bear the vision better for what they show us, but the cost to them is sometimes very great: suicides, insanity, the induced insanity of alcohol and drugs—these are not, I think, weaknesses or self-indulgences for such men, but rather a kind of sacrifice.

I want to speak finally about the response of love in two poets of our time, both now dead, who were friends of mine, Robert Frost and John Berryman. The attraction, or affinity, I felt for Frost and Berryman had a quality of discipleship. I knew them for my betters, that is. I'm proud that I had the instinct to recognize and learn from, if not my moral betters, at least my artistic largers. They gave to us, their brothers, great testimony of love. Let me say a poem of Frost's ("The Draft Horse") and part of a rejoinder to it by Berryman.

> With a lantern that wouldn't burn
> In too frail a buggy we drove
> Behind too heavy a horse
> Through a pitch-dark limitless grove.
>
> And a man came out of the trees
> And took our horse by the head
> And reaching back to his ribs
> Deliberately stabbed him dead.
>
> The ponderous beast went down
> With a crack of the broken shaft.
> And the night drew through the trees
> In one long invidious draft.
>
> The most unquestioning pair
> That ever accepted fate
> And the least disposed to ascribe
> Any more than we had to to hate.
>
> We assumed that the man himself
> Or someone he had to obey
> Wanted us to get down
> And walk the rest of the way.

It's a story, isn't it, about how love can turn evil around? It bears that witness.

Not long before his death, Berryman wrote a poem that appears in the posthumous book. It testifies to the communication of Frost's poem, in case anyone doubted that, and to the joy that we take, as loving animals, in the generosity of the artist. I read the opening and closing lines:

> Felled in my tracks by your tremendous horse
> slain in its tracks by the angel of good God,
> I wonder toward your marvelous tall art
> . . . .
>
> . . . .

> I said the same goddamn thing yesterday
> to my thirty kids, so I was almost ready
> to hear you from the grave with these passionate grave
> last words, and frankly Sir you fill me with joy.

I think what I learned from these two men, that I see witnessed in this exchange of poems, is that there is an appropriate response to anything that befalls us. It is a response that has to do with the love of our fellow man. It is prompted by a personal instinct of love. Its working is mysterious because this instinct is different in each of us. We are constantly being astonished, if we pay attention, at how differently people take their brotherhood. People who can't take it are non-people: we have cast-out names for them: monsters, zombies, self-lovers. And we can't dogmatize anything very important about love. What's true for me isn't exactly true for you: your instinct has another person for data. It would be dogmatic for me to assert that, at some level, the appropriate response to any crisis is affirmative, though I believe that. It would be dogmatic to assert that the prompting voice is creative, a manifestation of the creative force in the universe, but I believe that. Instinctively I have come to the role of an affirmative witness. Some lines I wrote this summer about another artist, a painter, are groping with this:

> Gnawed by a vision of rightness
> that no one else seems to see,
> what can a man do
> but bear witness?
>
> And what has he got to tell?
> Only the shaped things he's seen—
> a few things made by men
> a galaxy made well.

It's still more of a hunch than a creed. Richard Wilbur, who is a card-carrying Christian, said to me once that he prays to God because he has to have some place to take his gratitude. I suppose I am still at the stage where Mistress Quickly found herself at Falstaff's deathbed. "Now I (she says) to comfort him, bid him 'a should not think of God, I hoped there was no need to trouble himself with any such thoughts yet."

But I hope you will observe that for an agnostic I am a deeply superstitious man.

On Healing

My remarks this morning have to do with the problem of the ego, a matter on which most artists can speak with some authority, the problem of coming to grips with our own uniqueness. The vivid image of wrestling all night with an angel who at last gives a blessing, which we have just heard from Genesis 32, is nevertheless obscure enough to suggest that this is a mystery. I am going to take two literary characters, Childe Harold and Moses E. Herzog, as examples of men who look for themselves, though perhaps I will be speaking rather about Lord Byron and Saul Bellow.

The insight of healing that I want to suggest has to do with a perception about human nature that David Robb offered last Sunday, when his text was the verse from the Sermon on the Mount: Be ye therefore perfect, even as your father which is in heaven is perfect. He indicated that the word translated as *perfect* is more accurately rendered as *whole* or *complete,* a form of the Greek "telos." *Be ye therefore whole, as the Father is whole.* The rage to be whole is part of everyone's nature, but no two people will be whole in the same way. In Christian terms, I think this probably means that if you are to praise God in a way that is acceptable in his sight, it will be because you have come to the unique and probably lonely position which is called *you,* where no other will ever stand.

The work of Saul Bellow, the part of it I am familiar with, comprises a gallery of characters who share a passion for self-discovery, a rage to know who they are. This is true of Moses

Address delivered at Harkness Chapel, Connecticut College, January, 1977.

Herzog. You will remember we discover him, and leave him 350 pages later, in an abandoned house in the Berkshires, writing "endlessly, fanatically, to the newspapers, to people in public life, to friends and relatives and at last to the dead, his own obscure dead, and finally to the famous dead." He writes notes to himself, like this one: *"There is someone inside of me. I am in his grip. I feel him in my head, pounding for order. He will ruin me."* Another note says, *"That suffering joker."*

The immediate occasion for this wise, instinctive curative insanity is the collapse of his personal life—his second wife rejecting him for his closest friend. But in larger terms of his health, it is a function of his fate—as a human being and as a Saul Bellow character—that he has a fever to know who he is and what is his predicament.

This is something everybody has to find out, whether we find it out gradually or radically, once or a number of times, by some established exercise of our culture or religion, or (like Herzog) by a regime of solitary amazement—walking the maze of ourself until we learn its plan and our way out. "And when have we not preferred some going round / To going straight to where we are?" as Auden asks.

When we look for this identity, this *who am I, and what is my predicament?* the subjective part is as mysterious and as sacred as the objective. The same creator created both. The subjective part of the question can be phrased this way: what is in character for me? what are my characteristic responses? The objective part: what is an appropriate life for such a character on the planet earth in the late twentieth century? Asking these questions, Moses Herzog found himself at odds with many of the accepted responses of his time, and found that he had never recognized or declared that quarrel. In the last pages of the book we find this:

> To God he jotted several lines.
> *How my mind has struggled to make coherent sense. I have not been too good at it. But have desired to do your unknowable will, taking it, and you, without symbols. Everything of intensest significance. Especially if divested of me.*

Looking for Herzog, he finds a characteristic and alienating optimism in himself which is repelled by the spirit of his time: "But what is the philosophy of this generation?" he asks. "Not God is dead, that point was passed long ago. Perhaps it should be stated Death is God. This generation thinks—and this is its thought of thoughts—that nothing faithful, vulnerable, fragile can be durable or have any true power. Death waits for these things as a cement floor waits for a dropping light bulb. The brittle shell of glass loses its tiny vacuum with a burst, and that is that. And this is how we teach metaphysics to each other. 'You think history is the history of loving hearts? You fool! Look at these millions of dead. Can you pity them, feel for them? You can do nothing! They were too many. We burned them to ashes, we buried them with bulldozers. History is the history of cruelty, not love, as soft men think . . .' " This position offends his nature. Earlier he had spoken of such nihilism as a "mire of Post-renaissance, post-humanistic, post-Cartesian dissolution, next door to the Void . . . The very Himmelsteins" he cries out, naming the cynical and pragmatic lawyer who tries to befriend him, "the very Himmelsteins, who have never even read a book of metaphysics, were touting the Void as if it were so much salable real estate."

He writes to an old teacher of his, about the concept of inspiration whose loss he laments: *But you will be asking what has happened to "the inspired condition." This is thought (today) to be attainable only in the negative, and is so pursued in philosophy and literature as well as in sexual experience, or with the aid of narcotics, or in "Philosophical," "gratuitous" crime . . . (It never seems to occur to such "criminals" that to behave with decency to another human being might also be "gratuitous.") Intelligent observers have pointed out that "spiritual" honor, or respect formerly reserved for justice, courage, temperance, mercy, may now be earned in the negative by the grotesque.* Elsewhere he says, *"The world tells you to look for truth in grotesque situations."*

Beginning to know who he is not, through these pronounced dis-affinities, Herzog finds it not easy to say who, then, he *is*, what then is the truth. "A man may say, 'From now on I'm going to speak the truth,' " he complains. "But the truth hears him and runs away and hides before he's even done speaking."

What he settles for is that, first of all, he is a man of terrible curiosities: *Dear Professor Hoyle, I don't think I understand just how the Gold-Pore Theory works. How the heavier metals—iron, nickel—get to the center of the earth, I think I see. But what about the concentration of lighter metals?*

And next, that he is a man of promiscuous human concerns: *Dear Sirs, The size and number of rats in Panama City, when I passed through, truly astonished me. I saw one of them sunning himself beside a swimming pool. Another was looking at me from the wainscoting of a restaurant as I was eating fruit salad. Also, on an electric wire which slanted upward into a banana tree, I saw a whole rat-troupe go back and forth, harvesting. They ran the wire twenty times or more without a single collision. My suggestion is that you put birth-control chemicals in the bait. . . .*

And positively, he recognizes himself for an unfashionable optimist, he thinks hopefully:

"He now set down," Bellow tells us, "*Not that long disease my life but that long convalescence, my life.*"

He quarrels with the approved gloom. "*I venture to say Kierkegaard meant that truth has lost its force with us, and horrible pain and evil must teach it to us again. . . . I do not see this. Let us set aside the fact that such convictions in the mouths of safe, comfortable people playing at crisis, alienation, apocalypse and desperation, make me sick. We must get it out of our heads that this is a doomed time, that we are waiting for the end, and the rest of it, mere junk from fashionable magazines. Things are grim enough without these shivery games. People frightening one another—a poor sort of moral exercise.*"

This is not a philosophical sermon I am giving but something a good deal folksier. I don't urge Herzog's creed on anyone for whom it is not instinctive truth, though it is for me. Rather I urge the lonely work by which each of us must arrive at the *self* from which we can dispense all we have in life—love and attention. This self, this fabric of one's personal affinities, can be seen as an overcoming of foreign antibodies in the soul, the achievement of one's own healthy nature. "Things change but from what they are not to what they are," as Thoreau has it. Once located, to be forgotten. Once located, you are at the point where Herzog exclaims, *Everything of intensest significance. Especially if divested of me.*

What you do with the map of self, after you've found it, is the point I want to make finally about Lord Byron. In the poets we are reading this morning—Hopkins, Thomas Merton, Berryman—the divesting of self is so complete that the poetry is interchangeable with prayer.

The point I want to end with, about *Childe Harold*, which I take to be a more serious and perfect work than *Herzog*, is that Byron was never able, or only at the end of his life when he attempted to free the Greeks, to divest himself of the charm of being Lord Byron. He didn't even try. In 1818, Walter Scott (whose accomplishment is probably nearer to the scale of Bellow's—no mean writer, either of them) reviewed Canto IV of *Childe Harold's Pilgrimage.* He is generous to Byron, but his criticism is moral, and with his words I will finish this paradox, that *the ego is where you set out from, after you find it.* "Certain it is," Scott writes, "that whether as Harold or as Lord Byron, no author has ever fixed upon himself personally so intense a share of the public attention. His descriptions of present and existing scenes however striking and beautiful, his recurrence to past actions however important and however powerfully described, become interesting chiefly from the tincture which they receive from the mind of the author. . . . our ideas of happiness are chiefly caught by reflection from the minds of others, and hence it may be observed that those enjoy the most uniform train of good spirits who are thinking much of others and little of themselves . . . The poetry which treats of the actions and sentiments of others may be grave or gay according to the light in which the author chooses to view his subject, but he who shall mine long and deeply for materials in his own bosom will encounter abysses at the depth of which he must necessarily tremble. This moral truth appears to us to afford . . . a key to the peculiar tone of Lord Byron."

It was not a Victorian tone. It was a tone very like the prevailing one of our time, Harold's self-centered pessimism, where Scott can be charged with some of the dishonest cheerfulness we ascribe to the Victorians. But what Scott is saying, and what Bellow through his character Herzog is saying, about the ego is that after it has been discovered it should be divested. Dr. Johnson quoted a common saying of English physicians: "A cucumber should be well-sliced, and dressed with pepper and vinegar, and then thrown out as good for nothing."

V

Brief Reviews

Brief Reviews

The Dancing Bears

W. S. Merwin's second book, *The Dancing Bears,* maintains the standards of excellence that were widely remarked when he published *A Mask for Janus* two years ago. The chief virtue of his work, apart from an impressive virtuosity, seems to me to lie in its crystalline imagery. The clarity is not of language alone, nor of the details selected (which is how the Imagists were clear), but simply of the meaning of the images. A zodiac poem provides separable examples of how Mr. Merwin handles an image:

Virgo

Not so much as a song
In my most silver dream
Has ravished my ear.
Damage by beast and man
And by the scandalous sun
Sing out, but I am not there.

Sagittarius

All quarry flees. The arrow
Drawn always to my ear I still
Have not let fly, and yet they fall.

Or this Elizabethan grotesque from "Song of Three Smiles":

In "A Lot of Poems and a Bit of Theory," *Hudson Review* 2, no. 3 (Winter 1955). Copyright © 1955 by The Hudson Review, Inc.

> If you must smile
> Always on that other,
> Cut me from ear to ear
> And we all smile together.

The longest poem in the book is called *East of the sun and west of the moon.* It runs to more than 500 lines, and its marvelous imagery could sustain a colony of MLA scholars through a mild winter: to count the images, to demonstrate their unusual density, to show how they cooperate, and how they have been selected to a particular effect and from what Romantic and Renaissance sources. The poem is among Mr. Merwin's most successful. An allegorical narrative, it accommodates all the luxuriance and learning of his vocabulary and turns them to its purpose. The poems that fail to accommodate these characteristics (particularly the last two of three "Cansos" which end the book) have a verbosity which at worst chokes up the imagery:

> Or may the mind of heaven be a mind
> Of questions? As: is there not a country
> Or the negation of a country, where
> The mortal tree where the bird sang, the season
> Where you walked living, once existed only
> In their own deaths before their tides and branches
> Were from negation made?

I intend to quote unfairly: these images have a home in the poem, but by themselves they show what can happen when Mr. Merwin lets his language get away. Ezra Pound's influence is still strong on him, and occasionally results in rhetorical quagmires which Pound would never commit or condone. In the present volume only four poems, the first, the last two, and one in the middle called "The Passion," seem to me to be in any serious way impaired, and these by such faults as are not in the scope of any mediocre poet. The total effect of the book is of a major talent.

Images and Meaning: Chester Kallman and John Ashbery

The success or failure of contemporary poetry is often bound up with the use of subconscious imagery of what W. H. Auden calls, in introducing John Ashbery's book, "the inner mythological life." The powerful but private images of our dreams and daydreams, and the language natural to them, have been a main area of experiment for us.

Like rhythm, this imagery has a communicative force that is very hard to fix. We know that it can reinforce meaning, but some have held that it can, by itself, convey meaning. Poems and poets have failed by exaggerating the communicativeness of this resource—*The Waste Land* is at least partly such a failure—while the poets who did not experiment with it at all are somehow not modern poets. The dilemma is knife-edged: to avail oneself of an essential energy but avoid harmful obscurity. The greatest successes seem to have fallen to those who erred on the side of boldness, as is the way in this world.

Of the poets reviewed, Chester Kallman seems to have found the best solution. Three of the others tend toward their individual sorts of over-caution, while Mr. Ashbery is at times nothing short of foolhardy. A cautious practitioner myself, my sympathies may lie with those I call timid, but I am bound first to salute Mr. Kallman's golden mean and Mr. Ashbery's derring-do.

Storm at Castlefranco, Mr. Kallman's first book, reveals a rich and figurative imagination and an unusual talent for form and music. The unevenness of quality in his poems comes from their content. Some are needlessly protracted, like the long second sections of the title poem and "Elegy." Others, like the "Aria for an Emperor," are simply more carefully and musically wrought than their content seems worth. But where the material is a match for the craft, as often, there are some fine poems.

Mr. Ashbery's *Some Trees* starts off with three formidably

New York Times Book Review, April 15, 1956. Copyright © 1956 by The New York Times Company. Reprinted by permission.

obscure poems before we come to "The Instruction Manual," the first of eight or ten beautiful and accomplished poems. With the unsuccessful poems, it is a matter of the imagery not being objectified: they fail simply because the reader doesn't know what happens. If Mr. Ashbery has turned in dreams for his figures, he is remiss in telling us what he dreamt. A poem called "Sonnet," one of his parodies of conventional form, fails on repeated reading to supply essential transitions, and the reader is left with a few handsome lines and an enigma. The lucid poems, like "The Grapevine," "The Orioles," "The Painter," "He," show that Mr. Ashbery can exert his full force without such secrecy. At his best, he makes images like this:

> It was the toothless murmuring
> Of ancient willows, who kept their trouble
> In a stage of music.

Familiar Things Freshly Observed: May Swenson

The poet differs from other people in the significance he attaches to mere words, and in the pleasure he takes from them. In fact the mereness of a word, the unique and living energy which is something like its soul and often quite unlike its definition, is what he exploits. Words for him are not counters for the expression of thoughts and feeling but the very causes of thought and feeling.

May Swenson's original and charming poems seem to start from the premise that nothing is commonplace until matter-of-fact language and attitudes make it so. She leads the reader into fresh experience by riddles, a form of wordplay where the recognition of familiar things is delayed and insisted on. "Roused from napping in my lap / this nimble animal or five-legged star / parts its limbs sprat-wide." (Answer: her hand).

Miss Swenson uses the sounds of words slyly. Her rhymes

and echoes are often incomplete and internal, supplying (as we learned from her earlier book) organic rather than merely formal connections.

She has a distinct tone of voice that conveys muttered astonishment at what she sees and hears in the world. Her wizardry is sometimes diminished by private or precious associations. The poem called "Parade of Painters," for instance, is built of lines like "Titian heron leather pimento": what was sibylline elsewhere is pixie here. But *A Cage of Spines* is a very successful book and maintains great verbal originality.

Images and Reality

The word *academic* when applied to poetry, as in Jack Kerouac's fine phrase "gray-faced academic quibbling," is almost always derogatory. It remains for a poet like James Merrill with a tough, agile, literary mind to remind us that poetry, like the true academy, is a place to celebrate the mind.

When Merrill's *First Poems* appeared eight years ago his mind might have been considered merely an engaging and fanciful one. With the new volume it is clear that from behind a mask of wit and urbanity speaks a serious philosopher, perhaps even a moralist. The verbal elegance, and the Jamesian or Proustian world he draws his people and images from, are neither frivolous nor precious. They parallel and support grave statements about human experience. The artist's obligation to entertain us is fulfilled in a way that makes a constant metaphor: life beguiles us from its darker purposes in just this way, and gives us gifts with the same supple confusion.

The movement of Merrill's poems is often from a minute or refined observation to a suddenly much wider statement than we had expected, as though to warn us against trivial-looking objects. Things that appear to be precious in the false sense may be precious in the true, and both language and imagery act out this deception so that the reader has still the

New York Times Book Review, May 3, 1959. Copyright © 1959 by The New York Times Company. Reprinted by permission.

option of deceiving himself (and many will) that these poems are mere conceits.

A poem called "The Doodler," for instance, turns a telephone pad (and a rather class-conscious telephone pad, for Merrill is often obliquely concerned with the anomaly of a classless society) into the whole "white void" of life's possibilities. Other poems bring to the surface the clusters of imagery latent in the camera and the ouija board, while "A Timepiece" sees a pregnant woman swaying in a hammock as a mortal clock:

> Let us each have some milk, my sister smiled
> Meaning to muffle with the taste
> Of unbuilt bone a striking on her breast,
> For soon by what it tells us the clock is stilled.

In the "I" of the Poet: Snodgrass, Abse, and Gunn

It is not easy to talk about yourself in poetry and be sure that you will interest everyone. Think of some of those dead passages where Shelley or Wordsworth are more interested in themselves than they can get us to be. W. D. Snodgrass is a remarkable young poet who can make us feel that he is as interesting a subject as poetry affords. The poems in this first volume are carefully and conventionally made, but they keep saying things that are beautifully peculiar. In the end they establish a balanced, humorous, modest *persona* that is just about irresistible. A poem called "A Cardinal" opens:

> I wake late and leave
> the refurbished quonset
> where they let me live.
> I feel like their leftovers:
> they keep me for the onset
> of some new war or other
>
> . . . .
> I crash through underbrush,

New York Times Book Review, July 26, 1959. Copyright © 1959 by The New York Times Company. Reprinted by permission.

> beer cans and lovers' trash
> in search of my horizons
> of meadowlark and thrush.
> Yet near me, here, it's still.
> I carry a scared silence
> with me like my smell.

"Snodgrass is walking through the universe," he says in another poem, and everyone who likes poetry should be glad because this seems to be a smart new instrument for examining the universe.

Two English poets of equal interest with Snodgrass have been published here recently for the first time. Dannie Abse, who has been overlooked even in anthologies, writes in a dry, exact vocabulary about miraculous things. There seems to be something of Robert Graves's magic formula from "The White Goddess" underlying the poems that invoke or propitiate supernatural forces: "The Second Coming" (less ambitious philosophically but no less terrible than Yeats's) and "Verses at Night":

> Sleepless, by the windowpane I stare—
>   black aeroplanes disturb the air.
>   The lazar moon glares down aghast.
>   The seven branched tree is bare.
>
> Oh how much like Europe's gothic Past!
>   This scene my nightmare's protoplast:
>   glow of the radioactive worm.
>   Future story of the Blast?
>
> Unreal? East and West fat Neros yearn
>   for other fiddled Romes to burn;
>   and so dogma cancels dogma
>   and heretics in their turn.
>
> But my wife, now I lie quiet as a
>   thought of how moon and stars might blur,
>   and miles of smoke squirm overhead
>   rising to Man's arbiter;
>
> the grey skin shrivelling from the head,
>   our two skulls in the double bed,
>   leukaemia in the soul of all
>   flowing through the blood instead.

> "No," I shout, as by her side I sprawl,
> "No," again, as I hear my small,
> dear daughter whimper in her cot
> and across the darkness call.

Thom Gunn, whose second book is first to be published in America, is another poet who risks talking about himself, fully aware (in Dannie Abse's words) that "where any poet sings, the vulture hovers." Most of the poems in *The Sense of Movement* are in the first person and implement the epigraph, "Je le suis, je veux l'etre" and the line of a poem, "But I am being what I please." In "Lines for a Book" he defines a kind of realistic romanticism (with audible parody of one of Spender's youthful Marxist lyrics): "I think of all the toughs through history / And thank heaven they lived, continually."

It is a good tough stance for poems. The book is not uniformly successful in holding it. A poem to Yvor Winters, among others, is a little inflated in rhetoric. A strong candor about the self marks all three of these books at their best.

A Note on Richard Wilbur

There are states of closed-mindedness—for and against—which ought to disqualify a man from reviewing particular books, and I suppose I am as badly qualified to review Richard Wilbur's *Advice to a Prophet* as, say, Jack Kerouac would be. We get committed to certain positions to the point where we aren't even interesting, let alone objective. But having said this, here are some words of caution I put in a letter recently. If a poem can say, as poems do, *pay attention to life*, a poet must sometimes say of the work he admires, *pay attention to these poems*.

It seems to me that for people who know and care about Wilbur's work, this is just the excellent book they had hoped for and expected. For other readers it is something of a booby trap. It invites careless reading: how genteel this all is, they think, how cheerful and Episcopalian, how very damned elegant. But these accusations, the ones that are actually derogatory anyhow, are self-generated. The poems will not support them.

Wilbur's poetry, like a lot of good poetry, has always been about order in the universe. Nowadays perceptions of disorder, even the most casually observed ones, are somehow taken to be more *serious*. Wilbur's poetry (like most good art, could you say?) explores the human capacity for happiness. The human capacity for despair (not to be confused with tragedy) is very big now with a lot of artists, and even novelists and poets who are not gifted in despair sometimes feel impelled to fake it.

But grace of form, a sweet accuracy of speech, a passionate sense of purpose still comprise most of what we know about poetry. *Advice to a Prophet* strikes me as the strongest assertion yet, by this poet, that the universe is *decent,* in the lovely derivative sense of that word. Like that word, the book is unfashionably quiet in what it asserts, and subject to misuse.

These poems are the kind of booby trap that life itself mines our path with. A reticence is part of the riddle. We all ignore the world somewhat, each in his own dull way, but never except to our cost. These poems are the observations of a man who has a sharp eye and ear for moral order. You ask yourself whether some of the poets whose work proclaims that the universe has lately become unseemly are as observant as Wilbur, whether they have as much regard for the riddle itself, the subject of our song.

James Dickey's Poems

James Dickey's *Helmets* is set apart from the run of everyday competent verse by its content: the poems arise from experience that requires poetry to comprehend it. The absence of this sort of experience is what makes so much otherwise unex-

Partisan Review 32, no. 3 (Summer 1965).

ceptionable modern poetry dull—the poets seem to have gone out of their way, conscientiously, to make poems out of their own fine sensibilities. With Dickey, the facts of his poems, or the best ones, demand a poem, and even if these facts, this experience, is sometimes taken by inept strategy, the results are nevertheless real poems and the experience comes on unarguable and true.

Dickey sees things his own way, almost wilfully, and his strategy is to bear down until the reader receives the same intensity of vision. It is unusual for a poet to hold so pig-headedly to a solipsistic insight without becoming private or perverse. The method is best seen in four or five magnificent poems in this book that are too long to quote: "Cherrylog Road," about an adolescent love affair conducted in the violent ruin of an automobile graveyard; "A Folk Singer of the Thirties," which catches a character and an era in a vast, fierce metaphor; and the first and last poems in the book, among them. But it can be seen in small in the opening lines of "The Ice Skin":

> All things that go deep enough
> Into rain and cold
> Take on, before they break down,
> A shining in every part.
> The necks of slender trees
> Reel under it, too much crowned.
> Like princes dressing as kings,
>
> And the redwoods let sink their branches
> Like arms that try to hold buckets
> Filling slowly with diamonds
>
> Until a cannon goes off
> Somewhere inside the still trunk
> And a limb breaks, just before midnight,
> Plunging houses into the darkness
> And hands into cupboards, all seeking
> Candles, and finding each other.

I guess it is some corollary of James Dickey's concern for the facts of experience that make his verse so plain. The unrhymed lines tend to have three beats, and are sometimes cut up into regular but totally arbitrary stanzas—"The Ice Skin," for instance, alternates divisions of seven lines and three—none of them describing organic divisions of the poem. This plainness puts as much pressure on the verbal and rhythmic accuracy of the language as in free verse. Dickey seems to welcome this attention to his insistent, unadorned observations of experience which, through attention, becomes miraculous.

The poems and parts of poems that don't work are those where he is making heroic metaphors out of experience that doesn't come off on that scale. A poem about "Kudzu," for example, strikes me as badly overwrought, while other fine poems like "Springer Mountain" and "The Scarred Girl" are extended beyond the range of their own intensity.

But Dickey is in the clear as a poet. He knows a poem when one happens to him and, like a small number of his talented contemporaries—James Merrill and W. D. Snodgrass, for instance—he puts his name on it.

Formal Effects: Hecht and Dugan

The chance to praise these books by two poets I've long admired finds me again in quest of that reviewer's mare's-nest—something not too farfetched that will hold my comments together. The greatest apparent dissimilarity between the work of Hecht and Dugan is in their prosody: between the elegant symmetry of rhyme and stanza in *The Hard Hours* and the gaunt plainsong of *Poems 3*. Yet this cleavage is not a joined battle but rather a function of the poets' identities and concerns. These men work at opposite ends of a broad spectrum of formal effects, and the excellence of their books lies partly in a sureness of prosody.

The Hard Hours, coming thirteen years after Anthony Hecht's first book, releases with dramatic completeness a talent that was only hinted at in *A Summoning of Stones.* The

New York Times Book Review, December 17, 1967. Copyright © 1967 by The New York Times Company. Reprinted by permission.

truth is, the weak poems in the earlier book, and a few in the present one, are weakened by a mechanical sense of form. The strong and spacious poems that give the new book its character—poems like "A Hill," "Behold the Lilies of the Field," and "More Light! More Light!"—demonstrate how well Hecht understands the economy of his vision. He brings these poems to book by the most intense lyric control. Only in two poems in the new book do I feel the kind of cookie-cutter use of stanza that gave his first book a slightly frivolous effect. These are called "Ostia Antica" and "The Origin of Centaurs," and perhaps the very concerns of the poems suggest the brittleness of form. But observe how urgent and organic the stanza is in the opening of "Lizards and Snakes":

> On the summer road that ran by our front porch
>   Lizards and snakes came out to sun.
> It was hot as a stove out there, enough to scorch
>   A buzzard's foot. Still, it was fun
> To lie in the dust and spy on them. Near but remote,
>   They snoozed in the carriage ruts, a smile
> In the set of the jaw, a fierce pulse in the throat
>   Working away like Jack Doyle's after he'd run the mile.

Alan Dugan works at the other end of the spectrum. The freedom of his verse bodies forth a fierce, solipsistic freedom of spirit and vision. When his first book (which won the Pulitzer Prize in 1962) appeared, the English critic A. Alvarez called him "a poet utterly—and mercifully—without charm." But there is no lack of rhythm or of a certain Webern-like music, always deriving from the particular experience of the poem, as in "Poem":

> A man with a box walked up to a woman with a boy, gave the box to the boy, said, "Don't drop it for a change," and kissed the woman, sucking up her rosebud from her mudcolor. It bloomed. He said, "Let's go." They went, with technicolor haloes of the usual around them. Why? Because: They come from a star, live by its light, and burn with it here in the dark outside of the department store.

Hecht is probably the greater individualist. The best practitioners of the new freedom of prosody, poets like Dugan, Olson, Levertov, are more influential with the young than their craftier contemporaries like Hecht, Wilbur, Elizabeth Bishop or Berryman. But it is all craft, and one would be sorry to see dogma obscure that governing mystery.

A Life of Poetry

It is very hard to write the way Muriel Rukeyser does, using your life as the direct vehicle of apprehension, the poems the same thing as closest attention to your daily life. "The old poetic task is we have to invent our own lives," Allen Ginsberg put it.

"The fear of poetry is the / fear," she wrote many years ago. In the new book she asks, "Do I move toward form, do I use all my fears?" Clearly the experience of poetry is the cutting edge of the life of someone who speaks like that.

If you are not used to thinking of poetry the way Muriel Rukeyser does, her work can be hard to read. The reader must acquiesce, perhaps more openly than with more conventional poems. Many people seem to have trouble with this beautifully voiced verse. The omission of her work from large, intelligent, catholic collections like *The Norton Anthology of Modern Poetry* testifies to that. As an admirer of Miss Rukeyser for almost forty years, I would like to make this a review that will move the unconverted.

The title poem of *The Gates* is a sequence about her journey to Korea and her efforts on behalf of the young imprisoned poet Kim Chi Ha. One of the lyrics proceeds by direct report of a conversation, as has been the strategy of many of her political poems. The dialogue carries the speaker's point—all the rhetoric, the false rhetoric, comes from the South Korean official:

New York Times Book Review, September 25, 1977. Copyright © 1977 by The New York Times Company. Reprinted by permission.

The Cabinet minister speaks of liberation.
"Do you know how the Communists use this word?"
We all use the word. Liberation.

No, but look—these are his diaries,
says the Cabinet minister.
These were found in the house of the poet.
Look, Liberation, Liberation, he is speaking in praise.

He says, this poet, It is not wrong
to take from the rich and give to the poor.

Yes. He says it in prose speech, he says it in his plays,
he says it in his poems that bind me to him,
that bind his people and mine in these new ways
for the first time past strangeness and despisal.

It also means that you broke into his house and stole his
papers.
Here is another poem, about Lot's daughter:

Ms. Lot

Well, if he treats me like a young girl still,
That father of mine, and here's my sister
And we're still traveling into the hills—
But everyone on the road knows he offered us
To the Strangers when all they wanted was men,
And the cloud of smoke still over the twin cities
And mother a salt lick the animals come to—
Who's going to want me now?
Mother did not even know
She was not to turn around and look.
God spoke to Lot, my father.
She was hard of hearing. He knew that.
I don't believe he told her anyway.
What kind of a father is that, or husband?
He offered us to those men. They didn't want women.
Mother always used to say:
Some normal man will come along and need you.

When the Academy of American Poets recently gave her the
Copernicus Award ($10,000 to "a living poet in recognition of
the poet's lifetime work and contribution to poetry as a cultural

force"), the citation started: "From her first book, *Theory of Flight,* published when she was twenty-one, through her recent collection, *The Gates* . . . the work of Muriel Rukeyser has been committed to ideas of freedom." The concerns of her poetry and her life remain inextricable, as with a person who can only tell the truth and take the consequences. The poetry in this fine book moves toward form, using all her fears—it is crafted in that hard way.

VI

Interview

The Art of Poetry

William Meredith lives in Uncasville, Connecticut, just outside of New London, in a rustic nineteenth-century barn that he converted into a house a number of years ago. For many years, he lived about fifty yards away in the large house that stands on the wooded property, but he eventually sold it to friends and moved into a smaller space. He likes to say that he originally bought the property—which overlooks the Thames, the river that figures in so many of his most characteristic poems—in order to keep himself rooted. "I knew that I had found a wonderful place to live and work at Connecticut College and I wanted to keep myself from leaving." Although he recently retired from teaching, Meredith has been associated with Connecticut College since 1955, where, over the years, he has clearly been well taken care of by both colleagues and friends.

Meredith was born in New York City in 1919, graduated from Princeton University in 1940, and served as a naval aviator during the Second World War and the Korean conflict. He has published seven books of poems: Love Letter from an Impossible Land *(which was chosen by Archibald MacLeish in 1944 for the Yale Series of Younger Poets),* Ships and Other Figures *(1948),* The Open Sea and Other Poems *(1958),* The Wreck of the Thresher and Other Poems *(1964),* Earth Walk: New and Selected Poems *(1970),* Hazard, the Painter *(1975), and* The Cheer *(1980). He has also translated a volume of Apollinaire's poems and is currently co-editing a book of Bulgarian translations. Since 1964, he has been a chancellor of the Academy of American Poets, and from 1978 to*

Paris Review 95 (Spring 1985). The interview was held in April, 1983, three weeks before William Meredith's stroke. Edward Hirsch conducted and edited the interview and was assisted by Michael Collier.

1980 he was the Consultant in Poetry to the Library of Congress. In 1984, he was awarded one of the first Senior Fellowships of the National Endowment of the Arts.

On the day of the interview, a spring morning in 1983, Meredith was wearing a soft, bone-colored V-neck sweater with an open collar and brown corduroy pants. He looked decidedly nonprofessorial— casual enough to work in the garden, but also turned-out enough to sit and have cocktails with friends. The interview was conducted around a kitchen table in the dining area downstairs. It had poured the previous day, and there was still some evidence of moisture on the stone floor. Meredith seemed a little tired—he had suffered a major heart attack about a year before—but otherwise very much himself. Everything he says is informed by a sharp intelligence, a sly wit, a deep modesty, and a complex optimism. We overheard him tell a close friend on the telephone that morning, "We're in bad health, but high spirits."

You've said that you average about six poems per year. Why so few?

Why so many? Ask any reviewer. I remember a particularly wicked review of Edna St. Vincent Millay whose new poems weren't as good as they should have been: "This Millay seems to have gone out of her way to write another book of poems." You're always afraid of that. That could be said, I believe, of certain people's poems. So I wait until the poems seem to be addressed not to "Occupant" but to "William Meredith." And it doesn't happen a lot. I think if I had a great deal more time it would happen more often because I would get immediately to the typewriter. But it might happen eight times a year instead of six—not much more than that. I'll say this because it may be interesting or important: I think it is because poetry and experience should have an exact ratio. Astonishing experience doesn't happen very often. Daily experience is astonishing on a level at which you can write a poem, but astonishing experience would be the experience which is not astonishment of reality but astonishment of insight. It is for me, as a lyric poet, to make poems only out of insights that I encounter. Robert Frost used to say, "How many things have to happen to you before something occurs to you?"

How do you usually start a poem?

It starts with an insight which gets a few words close to the ground and then the words begin to make specific the insight. Once they start growing the words are seminal—I suppose it's like the bacteria of a growth. I can hardly remember a poem in which the words are not *particular* words, often very bleak, simple words. Once they are put down they are able to focus an idea. I have, I think, only once written a poem—and it's not a very good poem—which came to me literally as a dream that was decodable. It's about an eight or ten line poem and all I could say was, "That's what it said."

Your poems tend to have a sly, angular way of going at a subject, approaching it from the side rather than directly. Would you say something about that?

If it's so, it's the nature of the work that a poem is getting at something mysterious, which no amount of staring at straight-on has ever solved, something like death or love or treachery or beauty. And we keep doing this corner-of-the-eye thing. I remember when we were in training to be night fliers in the Navy, I learned, very strangely, that the rods of the eye perceive things at night in the corner of the eye that we can't see straight ahead. That's not a bad metaphor for the vision of art. You don't stare at the mystery, but you *can* see things out of the corner of your eye that you were supposed to see.

Do you think that writing a poem is a specific engagement of a mystery?

I would say exactly that. It is the engagement of a mystery which has forced itself to the point where you feel honor-bound to see this mystery with the brilliance of a vision. Not to solve it, but to see it.

Does this relate to the statement in your poem "In Memory of Robert Frost," that Frost insisted on paying attention "until you at least told him an interesting lie."

Well, he understood—and I'm afraid his biographer, Lawrence Thompson, does not understand—that at the higher reaches of our experience we don't know the things that we say, but we say that we do. That's the ultimate artistic lie. I tell you what I know today in a poem and I don't know it; in the first place it may not be true, and in the second place it may not be what I know tomorrow. Artistic truth is to declare, under torture, what the torturer does not want you to say, not what the torturer does want you to say. You try to tell the truth even though it's uncomfortable for everybody. When the hippies were talking about how the only two things you need to know about life is that you must love one another and not lie, they forgot to tell you that those are the only two really difficult things. We all know that's what we're supposed to do; it's much harder to love people than anybody ever tells you and it's much harder to tell the truth. Poets are professionally committed to telling the truth, and *how* do they tell the truth? They say something that isn't true. This is the slyness of art: if you tell enough lies, you're bound to say something true. I think my work is only as good as it is honest but as a data bank it's full of errors.

Is it fair to characterize The Cheer *as a work of sly survivals, a resolutely hopeful book?*

A resolutely hopeful book I think it is. The question of survival, in fact the process of survival, is something that either occurs or doesn't occur. It doesn't seem to be something that one deliberately does, but is a product of good instincts and good life. And quite right. Survival, in terms of the poems, has been such that I use them for making my way from one form of commitment to the next. I hope that the poems will lead me more directly to where I'm going and that I'll arrive directed only by instincts, social instincts.

In a memorial poem to John Berryman, "In Loving Memory of the Late Author of Dream Songs," you write that "Morale is what I think about all the time / now, what hopeful men and women can say and do." Why morale?

I suppose it seems to me that the priestly function of artists in a society is to administer spiritual vision and that the obvious deficiency of a fragmented and confused society is in confidence. I use morale partly in quotation marks because I first became aware of the word in the military. Muriel Rukeyser pointed out to me that there was a certain General Euleo whose title was "Chief of Morale" and we thought that very funny. I was in the Navy so long that I have to remind myself that's a humorous title. But like General Euleo, I see the need for keeping the morale of the troops high. At one point it was in the papers that Congress had discovered large shipments of dice were being made to the troops overseas, and General Euleo explained that they were parts of a Parcheesi set they had not been able to requisition and that the whole thing would keep morale high. That's like *The Cheer*. My real concern is, in the first place, that we ought not to be solemn and, in the second place, the response to disaster, even cultural disaster, is an impersonal one and the personal obligation is to mental and spiritual health. Of course, it always has been.

In "Hazard's Optimism" you also note that Hazard is "in charge of morale in a morbid time." Is that one of the poet's responsibilities?

I would suppose so. In a happy time, like Elizabethan England, the poet is probably involved in reminding people that they're all going to come to a bad end. Nowadays, you try to keep people from precipitating their own bad ends.

Playfulness and humor also seem to be an integral part of your poetic stance.

I first learned about playfulness from W. H. Auden, who talks about it all the time. But the example of playfulness I found in Frost was the great attraction of Frost for me. I could see that he played games with words, a sort of Hide and Seek with the reader, and therefore the poems were never as earnest as English teachers said they were. People who are basically humorous are constantly misunderstood in an instructive way. My social career is littered with ill-calculated humor. One doesn't want to say, "I live on the verge of despair and terror and I'm perfectly safe because I'm roped off by humor and good cheer." But sometimes, it's the only way to talk about things. Here is an example: in the Navy, when we were flying, instead of saying, "Take care of yourself," people would say, "Don't crash and burn." I don't know how funny it was, but we thought it was hilarious. Still, there were some people who forgot and didn't take care of themselves and did just that. Humorlessness is a positively morbid quality that certain people have. This is not the same as not being witty, it's not the same as not using humor in a particular instance. It's a solemnity which puts blinders on your awareness of ridicule and absurdity. I'm always suspicious of humorlessness. When you see the pictures of Hitler jumping up and down and laughing with glee over the conquest of France you see a somewhat disoriented human being whose life has had a deficiency of laughter. It's almost a snickering.

Frost has had an enormous impact both on your life and on your work. What do you think in particular that you learned from him?

When we were in Tucson on a visit once he quarreled with me about something. I guess indeed I quarreled with him on a statement of dignity, and in making up he said, "I brought you along on this trip so you could see a little how I take things." That's also his definition of style: style is how a man takes himself. I think I learned—it's not a very precise answer but it's precisely what I learned on the page and from the person—that that was the way I would like to take myself. I think one of the reasons I am so quick to rush to the defense of Frost, who after all was not any nicer than most of us, is that I wouldn't mind being as nice as he was. He took things very generously and magnanimously. His language fascinates me because he lived within his means in language, like an old man. There's never a single word that seems wanting, not a single word that seems to call attention to itself in a pretentious way.

Is this an attitude from life which applies itself to how a man takes his poems?

One time he said, in connection with his youth and his mother's life, "People used to call us riff-raff. They never knew what riff-raff I am." I take that to be his form of modesty, which is puzzling to people who think he was vain. I think it has to do with his making do with his human and verbal resources, knowing exactly what the best you could do was and doing it.

What are your favorite Frost poems?

"The Vanishing Red," "Directive," "Spring Pools," "The Birthplace."

In his poem "For John Berryman," Robert Lowell writes, "Really we had the same life, / the generic one / our generation offered." How much do you think of yourself as a poet who belongs to a particular generation?

I feel myself of that generation because I had the good luck to know those poets. As far as our experience being similar, I think the responses of people like Richard Wilbur or Elizabeth Bishop are different from the responses of Berryman and Lowell, and Randall Jarrell's was different still. So that while I'm sure we had basic encounters with history that nobody else had, we took them differently. I believe Lowell is right in associating himself so closely with Berryman. Berryman associated himself closely with Lowell, and both of them with Jarrell, although if you look at Jarrell's work, you wouldn't know that there was any relation. It's one of my theories that Jarrell is probably the most useful poet of the three.

Why?

His poems are accessible to people who are not trained readers. You have to train yourself to read Berryman, though it's very much worthwhile. I would say to somebody who wants to read Berryman what Nabokov said about Pushkin: "Learning Russian is a small price to pay for reading Pushkin." But every other poem in Jarrell's *Complete Poems* is accessible to somebody who is not a trained reader of poetry. It is just interesting, attractive, and human. Anybody who can read a short story by O. Henry can read a poem by Jarrell.

You've written about Jarrell, "The poems he left behind seem to me to speak in the most compassionate voice of any of his generation." Is compassion the virtue you most prize in Jarrell? What about his acid wit?

His wit was splendid. I think it's twice splendid because he almost never used it except when appropriate. He used it to detect falsehoods, to deflate intolerable pretension. The reason I think it's less important than compassion is that it is a more common thing in our time. Jarrell wasn't any wittier than Tom Wolfe, say. Also, I lived in mortal fear of him. Why not? He gave a talk in 1962—one of his modest talks where he was assessing fifty years of modern poetry in fifty minutes at the Library of Congress—and at the end he said, "And then there is another larger group of poets who, so to speak, came out from under Richard Wilbur's overcoat." It was a reference to Dostoyevsky's famous comment on Gogol, "We all come out from under Gogol's overcoat,"* and it made me feel that I was in that category of poets. I thought then that I would just like to get through life without ever attracting his attention.

When did his poems start to interest you, or influence your work?

I can date it precisely: it was when I reviewed *The Lost World* in 1964. I read his work very carefully then and with great admiration. Mary Jarrell tells me that he was very pleased with the review and when I saw him with Lowell he treated me with respect, though I can't imagine that my poems interested him

---

*Dostoyevsky's comment refers to Gogol's story, "The Overcoat."

very much. But, really, it's the vertebra that I think mine could nearest approach. His and John Crowe Ransom's are the two works most like the works that are my mind's.

Is Ransom one of your models?

Ransom is a bad model in the sense that he wrote his book of poems and then didn't do much, didn't grow as a poet, didn't have much more to say. I just would like to have forty poems as good as that to call my own, that's what I mean. Also, I would like to have such original insights.

Lowell's poem "Morning after Dining with a Friend" describes a dinner which you had with Lowell near the end of his life. It also refers to your first meeting. How accurate is the poem, and would you talk about your relationship to Lowell both as a person and as a poet?

The poem, like everything he wrote, is terribly accurate, but the remark about the language of the tribe is changed in mode from declarative to optative. What I actually said was, reading the new batch of poems he gave me that evening, "I feel that with every book you have come a little closer to the language of the tribe." And that's what I say I said in my poem. I have it in his own handwriting that night "to move a little closer to the language of the tribe if we could." So he thought—and he may have been correct—that I was saying: "You've got a long way to go." I wouldn't have the insolence to say that then or now, but what I might have meant was, if you can write this much more accessibly every year you will eventually become as useful as Frost as well as as great as Lowell. That's what I must have had on my mind but I surely didn't urge him to do anything. It's just not my style to urge people to do things. But the account of our meeting is correct as I remember it. I was a member of the Metropolitan Opera Club in those days and we met there—it must have been in 1954—when he was a guest of his friend, Bob Giroux. I had on a uniform because you had to wear either evening clothes or a uniform, and it was easier to put on a uniform. Very soon after that he came to give a lecture at Connecticut College. He was the house guest of his friend Mackie Jarrell (Jarrell's first wife), and I spent the evening with them. In that same winter (1955–56) the Lowells invited Mackie and me to visit them at their cottage. I remember at the end of the visit he said, "I feel this has been a momentous meeting." We stayed friends through the years. Nobody had any trouble staying friends with Cal. He was an extremely loyal and generous man.

Would you gloss the last lines from your poem "Remembering Robert Lowell": "To punish the bearer of evil tidings / it is our custom to ask his blessing. / This you gave. It dawns on each of us separately now / what this entails."

To me that line is interesting because it was written under the influence of Lowell. It is not a meritorious line and I'm not sure I'm entitled to tell you what it means any more than I could tell you what it means when I paraphrase a Lowell line. He has the gift for that kind of meaningful inversion of myth. He told us these things about ourselves and we gave assent to the things that he said. And the blessing we asked was: after such knowledge, what forgiveness? And now each of us, reading Lowell, sees what is the appropriate response to that terrible lucid vision of twentieth-century America. He's a much more American poet than anyone ever probably knew. It is ultimately a very American manifestation—think of Henry James or T. S. Eliot—to look over the shoulder of the educated person to see what we can salvage from our past to regain our direction in the twentieth century.

So Lowell is particularly American because of his entanglement with American history?

Yes, he was very conscious of that. I'm very conscious of it too, but it seems to me that one doesn't talk about it. It annoys me to have been called "aristocratic" when the truth is I have a very deep sense of the commitment of eighteenth-century settlers to this country, all of my ancestors having come to this country before 1800. I don't need to talk about it, what I need to do is find out what's appropriate and do it. Also, my name isn't Lowell. My name is a considerable name: it was on a piece of paper currency in the nineteenth century, a ten-cent fractional note. But this is not the kind of bragging that Lowell did and it's certainly not the kind of bragging I would do; it's only that I'm aware of these things and not ashamed of them. I only wonder what possible usefulness they have—what sense of that kind of history can go into a modest man's modest work.

John Berryman's thirty-sixth "Dream Song" is dedicated to you. It begins, "The high ones die, die. They die. You look up and who's there?"; and it ends with a parenthetical "(Frost being still around.)" What's your attitude toward the poem? Does it set up a dialectic that's important to you: the doomed poet against the poet as survivor?

I have a version of "The high ones die" which he wrote out for me at Bread Loaf that says, "The great ones die." He was thinking specifically of the fact that Faulkner and Hemingway had died. He was thinking about mortality and not suicide. He wasn't thinking that the line means "even the high ones die"—rather that it's a bad time to be a high one. "Frost being still around" means the survival of certain high ones is to be thought of, too. The parenthesis probably means to suggest the jeopardy of age. To me the poem was a statement of praise like those other poems he wrote about Frost afterwards, when Frost died. He was saying that we live in a terrifying world where the great poets are being taken from us. It's true that we can't see anybody on the American horizon now who is quite the size of Faulkner or Frost. We are aware of all other kinds of inferiority and this is added to the hazards of the morale. It would be nice if a Robert Frost or a William Faulkner were regularly produced at twenty-year intervals.

Three of the poems in The Cheer *deal with Berryman, "Dreams of Suicide," "In Loving Memory of the Late Author of Dream Songs," and "John and Anne." Berryman seems to be a key figure to you both as a person and as a poet. Would you talk about your relationship to him?*

He and I were more familiar than I ever felt myself to be with Auden, Frost, or Lowell. I was intimate with Lowell but not familiar. We were close friends and the warmth was there, but my mind is not of the size or shape of Lowell's and I was always aware of this. Berryman was wonderful: anything you didn't know that was necessary to follow his argument he would fill in. He didn't expect me to be anything but bright. I have a postcard from him, written when I was doing a piece about the sonnets at his request. I had asked him to identify a source. He wrote me back with the information and the rest of the postcard says, "Really, Meredith, what will you pretend not to know next?" I was familiar with him. You had to accept his undignified behavior in a way that was comfortable for him and you had to do that naturally. Not everybody could do it. I naturally felt that his dignity was never lost. I knew when the alcohol was taking over. I always knew that he was misspeaking himself, rather than saying something wrong. He was saying something in human need. He understood that and relied on it.

Do you think there's been too much emphasis on his tormented biography?

In the sense that John Haffenden's biography of Berryman and Ian Hamilton's biography of Lowell are not the proportions of the men's lives. Most of the time that I was with Lowell and Berryman, they were happy. They had the happiness of seriously engaged, useful people. That's the impression that I think a biography ought to give. It's our style now that a poet is taken seriously in proportion to his tortures, particularly if his tortures can be blamed on himself. I think it's inappropriate as a value judgment and inappropriate to apply to those two in life. Remember they gave of their company; they gave a great deal. This is partly what I was bitching about in the poem called "The Cheer." We're convinced that you shouldn't smile in public because people are being killed in El Salvador today. I am no less gravely sad about history than the solemn people are. But part of my response is to try to reverse it personally because there is dignity in our response and our response is not self-pitying or entirely angry, but a historical one. There is a historical answer to what befalls us and I think the people of good morale have better sense about how to respond.

Does Meredith's Hazard owe anything to Berryman's Henry, the protagonist of Dream Songs, *beyond the fact that they're both working at a time when, in words you quote from Berryman, "The culture is in late imperial decline"?*

I think it owes something in the sense of the playfulness of the character. I put three of those poems together (they may have appeared in a magazine) and sent them to Berryman and they didn't interest him at all. He was polite about them but I think that all he could see was that anything I could do he had done better. Maybe that clarified for me that I ought to distance myself more in the poem from the diction of Henry. I showed one of the poems to Mackie Jarrell and she said that she didn't like the lines. She didn't say they were from Berryman, but they were conscious attempts to fake his style. I think it does owe something to him in the freedom of colloquial speech, as in his concern about "lay" and "lie," his use of "ceremony-wise." All of which, I suppose, if the poem were to live one hundred years, would have to be glossed: "In those days there was a difference between the verb 'lie' and 'lay'; and in those days it was considered barbarous to use the suffix '-wise.' "

There is a powerful impulse in your work to move beyond the misgivings, grievances, and despair of so many of your contemporaries. Do you see your work as a dialogue or as an alternative to the work of contemporaries like Lowell and Berryman?

I see it as a dialogue because it relates me to the writers that I admire and know personally. We have different things to say in our poems, we have different visions, so that, in essence, it's a dialogue. I don't think their visions are wrong and mine is right. Mine is corrective of one thing and theirs is corrective of another. It's the distortion of art. I distort to see the truth and they distort to see the truth.

And yours is a more optimistic distortion?

It really is, and I think it comes from having been a closet Christian all my life. I believe in salvation.

Although much of your work is concerned with moral purposes, it does not strike one as being blatantly religious. In fact, the speaker in most of your poems seems to offer the consolation of a well-honed agnosticism. But in a recent poem, "Partial Accounts," you write, "Growing older, I have tottered into the lists / of the religious, tilt." Is this incontrovertible evidence of a conversion?

No, I would simply say I came out of the closet. My belief is a little clearer to me now and I feel that I ought not to hide it. You know that the best Christian writers don't talk about it as though they were trying to sell you a product. I think of Gerard Manley Hopkins. All the good criticism of Hopkins is written by agnostic Jews and brainwashed nuns who understand that the poetry is true and the truth is what will prevail as a religious example. I say that I'm careful not to practice Christianity conspicuously. But I want to pay attention through the medium of religion. I'm going to give a talk in chapel this month and my theme is going to be that the greatest imaginative accomplishment of the human imagination is atheism. It's the only thing that man has thought up creatively without the help of God. It's a short course but it's a very interesting one. It's sort of like concrete poetry; after you've gotten to the bottom of atheism, you don't have very much left. It's an experiment that has run its course. It is my feeling that all the other works of the imagination are derivatives of the creative imagination of a creator. I don't believe in being very doctrinaire and when I'm among the humanists in Bulgaria, what I say is, "Indeed man isn't all the work of God. Indeed there is no reason that he need refer to God." But that's where I see it coming from.

Is it accurate to say that in recent years your work exhibits a greater willingness to speak to public subjects?

I hope so. I think this had partly to do with my having to think of myself as a public servant again after twenty-five years of not being in public service. I considered myself a public servant when I was in the Navy. Afterwards, I wondered what a public servant does in the role of a poet. When I went to Washington as the poet to the Library of Congress I had a chance to see what could be done with a large audience. Thinking about what happened at the Library of Congress, the chain of artists that one follows there, you see that Americans do have some slight sense of the public function of the poet. It's nice that the Library of Congress has that. It's the branch of Congress that has literary opinions.

In poems like "Politics" and "Nixon's the One" (from Hazard, the Painter) *and "On Jenkins' Hill" and "A Mild-Spoken Citizen Finally Writes to the White House" (from* The Cheer), *you develop an unusual civic stance for a contemporary poet, a kind of "poet as concerned citizen" approach to the political scene. Does that characterization seem accurate to you? And does this attitude signify a new kind of openness or political engagement in your work?*

I believe that it represents an openness that I've always felt and acted on but never found much way, before this, to talk about in poetry. The lyric poem is so often private. For example, my intention in writing "The Wreck of the Thresher" was to write a "public" poem about my feeling of disappointment in the hopes of the United Nations. When I was writing that poem (and I kept all the drafts of it because I wrote it as a sort of dialogue with my friend Charles Shain, who was here that summer without his wife, being the President of the College; I would leave the draft off for him in the morning and he would scribble notes on it and send it back), I remember seeing it change from a rather pretentious public statement to the very private statement it turned out to be. It occurred to me that this is simply a demonstration of what Auden said in *The Dyer's Hand,* that we don't trust a public voice in poetry today. I would say that my concern about politics is precisely the concern of a Joan Didion or a Denise Levertov but that my stance is very different, so it doesn't appear to be the same. There is a spectrum of political opinion and a spectrum of political involvement. I stand with regard to involvement where those two women stand, but in the political spectrum I'm much more Jeffersonian—I'm nearer the middle.

Your friend, the poet Muriel Rukeyser, had a great sense of the poet's social responsibility.

Yes. I was never as clear about that as she is. I suppose I'm halfway between Muriel Rukeyser, whose every breath was socially responsible, and James Merrill, who pretends not to read the newspapers. Somewhere in the middle is where most artists belong. I sign a lot of things, I send a lot of funny dollars off. Every four years I have a kind of knee-jerk political life. But I can't compare myself to Muriel in that, except insofar as I pay attention to the things that need to be done in the world. One doesn't miss Vietnam and El Salvador.

You have several poems dedicated to Rukeyser. In what way was she influential and important to you?

She was the first poet that I knew personally. I knew her when I was still an undergraduate. She was a very amazing human being and any traces of honesty in my life come from having seen how beautifully honest she was in administering her life and her poetry without any separation—you couldn't get a knife between those two things with her. And my poems are very different from my life, alas. But I understand that that's one of the things you work at when you hope to get better as a poet. The real influence was her human model of what a poet could be. Clearly, our poems have almost nothing in common. But we liked each other's poems, which is an important form of attraction to one's own insufficiency. You like people who can do things you can't do.

You mentioned James Merrill before. One of his chief poetic models is also one of yours: I'm referring to Auden.

I see more of it in my work than in Merrill's. Of course, the wandering spirit of Wystan Hugh Auden prevails in Merrill's trilogy. That spirit is charming and very genuine: it's clearly coming directly. But in my work there is a lot of Auden that nobody could see except me. I don't know how to tell you what it is. In my mind, my playfulness is a lowbrow American version of his Oxford playfulness. Two of the lines in my poem "About Opera"—"What dancing is to the slightly spastic way / Most of us teeter through our bodily life"—seem Audenesque to me, and I think Auden liked them. I don't know exactly what I mean by Audenesque. It's like Kafka; it's a totally subjective feeling of how you play with language until you get to something spooky.

It must have been particularly exciting to first encounter Auden's poems.

It was terribly exciting. It seemed like an appropriate way of handling a new experience of one's own and, oddly enough, what all of us sensed was the Marxism of it. And that's what Auden rejected with the style itself. It was an early mannerism, almost, with him, of such originality and so appropriate for the matter. Of course, as soon as the Marxist matter ceased to concern him the manner went with it. But at the time of my college education, the big events, the El Salvador and Vietnam, were the Scottsboro case and the Spanish War. We were very aware of right and wrong and of the correctness of Marx's diagnosis of why wrong was wrong, if not always of why right was right. The other thing—and this is pointed out very well by Edward Mendelson in his book about Auden and somewhat less well but interestingly by Humphrey Carpenter—is that Auden was trying to disguise his private life in those poems so he had to invent a code. The code language applies both to the underground camaraderie of revolutionaries and the underground camaraderie of homosexuals. I was such an underground homosexual that I didn't even talk to myself, let alone anyone else, about it. But I could see that there was something in his language that was appropriate to my intense repressions. I think I picked it up in his short line poems.

Both you and Auden share a deep passion for the opera. How is that passion related to your poetry?

Not directly at all. I think it might say something about the mystique of form, artifice and form, that we both subscribe to. The preposterous Italian opera seems just as realistic to me as Theodore Dreiser now, in the sense that it describes exactly what I see life to be like. And that's pretty peculiar. An important fact about this, which Auden points out, is that we were both fortunate enough not to know anything about opera until we were formed as poets. So it can't have been any influence, but an affinity.

Would you say something about the opera criticism that you wrote for the Hudson Review?

I would say it was lucky that I was never found out.

Did Auden's work change your sense of Yeats's poetry?

Something changed it. Auden supplanted Yeats as an influence at the time. The opposite side of me from what Frost was nourishing had been nourished by Yeats, and that was the intellectual side. I found Yeats intellectual but I found his poems cerebral. A lot of it wasn't actually sustaining with Yeats. Yeats wasn't a whole lot brighter than Tennyson, the only two poets that I feel myself equal to intellectually. It's a very interesting thing about Auden that he was able to wrestle Yeats to the mat by 1939, and pay these enormous respects to him without any animosity because he could see there was no competition.

One of the Yeats poems that crops up in your work is "The Wild Swans at Coole."

I like the early minor poems enormously. I think my favorite Yeats poem is "Upon a Dying Lady." It is a very small poem, not in length but in grasp, and it is so elegantly worded.

Is it the high rhetoric that you object to in Yeats's poetry?

I don't object to it at all. I find "Sailing to Byzantium" a wonderful piece of music, but it no longer seems to have any model value for me. As I look back, it was only an affectation to think that it ever did. I remember how odd I felt showing Frost my little poem "To a Western Bard" where the last paragraph starts "Or our own great poet's rage / Yeats. . . ." Frost must have wondered why the hell I didn't say Frost. And twice would he have wondered, once because he was greater than Yeats in his own mind—or maybe not, but competitive—and twice because he must have known that Yeats was no place for me to be whoring around.

Throughout your work, you continually exhibit and also prize the civic virtues of modesty and formal restraints. Why do you think these are so important?

They seem to work for me and I think they're neglected. They're a small part of the picture, but they're a part of the picture that, first of all, isn't talked about very much and, secondly, that I think I know something about.

In the fourteen new poems in Earth Walk, *in* Hazard, the Painter, *and in* The Cheer, *the style seems a little more casual and idiomatic, roomier and more meditative, less metrically concentrated. Do you feel that after your* Selected Poems, *your work has been evolving a new mode and style?*

I guess I have the poet's antennae for what's going on in the medium. I've adapted the kind of formalism that is mine with the sensibility for formalism that's abroad in the United States. I would say if you want to see how this happens you can look at the work of Berryman or Lowell and see at what point they stopped using initial capitalization and semicolons and exclamation points. My form, insofar as it's subconscious and instinctive, is responsive to the colloquial, by which I mean in this case the colloquial of the genre. What constitutes the very problematic is audibly different from what constituted my speaker's voice. I believe that I will continue to write poems that are shaped like sonnets and villanelles, but I will write them in a way that sounds to me like the modern version.

It sounds like this opening up is a little unwilling.

It is the opening up of a poet who owes as much responsibility to the tradition as to the new and the novel. In that sense, I'm not willing to modify forms which seem to me very energized still. I want to use them now as they were used then, which is to say, to change them.

In a prefatory note you refer to Hazard *as a "characterization" and your publisher describes it as "a miniature novel in verse." Is your sequence trying to regain some of the large territory that poetry has lost to prose fiction?*

Rather, I think, an attempt to concentrate on the dramatic virtue of the lyric poem. It comes from contemplating for years Frost's remark, "Everything written is as good as it is dramatic." I felt that many of the experiences that I wanted to comment on would be more interesting if I could give them to somebody else with a different opinion. Take Hazard's problem with his friend's homosexuality: it's the reverse of my problem. I belive in equal rights for heterosexuals. I have a lot of problems with it, and this is a way of getting at them. I was thinking really about, in that relationship, what I must look like to Lowell. Mostly, I'm Hazard in the sequence, but in the poem "Wholesome" I'm Elliott and Lowell is Hazard. But the poet has no character in the sense that he is interchangeable.

Apollinaire, a poet you've translated particularly well, talks about the long quarrel between tradition and innovation. Is that quarrel germane to your work?

I'd rather agree with anybody than quarrel, you know. I think I would say, "Guillaume, you're perfectly right." That doesn't help me. I have no quarrel with tradition, as all of my enemies have pointed out. I think there is no point in striving to be modern or original, because I live now and I am unique. Not terribly unique, but God thinks I'm unique, and in that consists my originality. My modernity consists of the dates of birth and death. So that I don't have this battle with tradition. I feel terribly grateful for any insight that tradition gives me as to what we're about. One of the things that poets sometimes forget is that—by their job specification—they are dealing with the most conservative force in culture, that is, language. I believe that my sense of tradition is limited by my ignorance, not by my conservatism. I would like to be more indebted to Spenser but I haven't been able to get through *The Faerie Queene* yet.

What do you think you learned from Apollinaire?

I learned to lie back more fearlessly on my subconscious. I think the little poem I wrote called "For Guillaume Apollinaire" is an attempt to say how wonderful it was not to be held accountable for a rational organization of the poem, but simply to feel and to say in English, "Honest to God, that's what Apollinaire said." I'll stick up for him even though it would not have come to me naturally. I think I have one of the most constricted imaginations of any good poet of our time and he had the most liberty in imaginations. It was a helpful distortion. Actually, if I had known about this device I would have started to translate poets like Rilke before. Rilke may be the poet to whom I'm most completely insensitive. I can see what he's doing, but it doesn't make much sense to me. My dream life is as orderly as my waking life.

Of course, Jarrell was a great Rilkean.

Lowell was not and Berryman was not. But none of us will say a word against him. One of my favorite stories about this is the story that Charles Rosen tells about Richard Strauss. He was advisor to Mahler's widow, who had set up the notion of a foundation with her husband's money, and she gave it to composers who needed money. They wrote her and told her why they wanted it—you didn't have to explain how many boats you owned or how much booze you consumed. You just said what you wanted the money for. She consulted Strauss about Arnold Schoenberg and Strauss said, "I've heard some of his recent work and for my part, I think you would be better off in Vienna shoveling snow than giving him the money. But we never know what posterity will say, so you had better give it to him." That's the way I feel about Rilke.

Some of the poems in The Cheer *revolve around a single, central, and somewhat mysterious idea. I'm thinking of poems like "Parents" and "Not Both." Would you say something about how these two poems were written?*

I'd love to tell you the story about "Parents" because it occurred one time after I'd gone to a Thanksgiving dinner where a couple I'm very fond of had three surviving parents. The three parents seemed to me valid, charming, interesting people, about my own age, and to their children they seemed, as parents normally do, embarrassing, stupid, tedious, albeit lovable. I saw my friends suffering and I remembered such suffering. The poem says essentially, "It is in the nature of things that one's own parents are tacky, and this should give you compassion because your children will find you tacky." The poem came out of that particular experience. "Not Both" came from the fact that I was entrusted, unfairly, as one is often entrusted, with a secret by someone who then said, "Probably I shouldn't have told you this, because I know that you don't have the character to keep a secret." I thought, okay, that's a dare, I will. I don't have the character to keep a secret and in this one case I will keep a seret and I won't tell it to anyone. The other examples in the poem are unresolved questions about people I know. I don't know whether one is a suicide, I don't know if one was having an incestuous love affair, and not ever knowing that is almost the same as it not ever having happened. Two things can happen and one did, and I don't know which one it is. And then the final thing is Pascal's wager: Somebody knows, or nobody knows, the answer to these questions.

The final line is a comment on that: "One of those two appalling things is true too."

Some people don't see how I use the word "cheer." I'm cheerful because I'm able to say that, to see that, and live. That's all I'd lose. Those are not the rules that I myself would have chosen. But we accept this wager from God, or not from God, and we don't despair. We assent.

What does it mean to say, as Thoreau does and as you affirm, that things change, but from what they are not to what they are?

Well, any time people ask me about the difference between the poems in *The Cheer*, formally or in content, from my earlier work, my impulse is to say that I'm more sure of what is in character for me now than when I was thirty-three, and the poems are what is in character for me. I have changed, like Thoreau's aphorism, only by sloughing off that which is not in character for me. I would have loved to write like Yeats or Matthew Arnold or Eliot at one time, but in terms of what's shown to me, I don't see in those spectrums, I don't see in that way or in those rhythms; so it was inappropriate, insofar as I imitated those people, to imitate that which is not in character. It was probably in character for me all along to imitate Wordsworth and Frost and Auden.

Theodore Roethke once said, "In spite of all the muck and welter, the dark, the dreck of these poems, I count myself among the happy poets." Do you want to be one of the happy poets?

I would like *The Cheer* to seem like someone who would say, "Yes. Without any reservations, I say yes." I speak about other things with reservations: things that I would want to change, things that I wish hadn't happened, things that we need to do and that we're not doing. But there are people who involuntarily give off an aura of "No," and those seem to be the people I quarrel with. It is inevitable to quarrel with that which you consider damaging in life.

In your introduction to a selection of Shelley's poems you wrote, "Art by its very nature asserts at least two kinds of good—order and delight." Do you still believe that?

I think I would say it more carefully.

What do you think you'll write next?

I think that at the rate that I go I will probably continue writing poems that synthesize or readdress some of the things I've seen in terms of the experience of my life. I'm not a quick study. I learn the things that are important in life very slowly and often more than once. The only thing the poet has to say is how he got an insight into what everybody already knows. I'll be trying to write poems that are generally accessible and attractive. And more and more I think happiness is the way that my poems go and the way that people take them, taking them as unpretentiously as they're offered. I am very happy about my relationships with students and friends, and I have this wonderful sense that my obligation comes from being privileged to write poems.

UNDER DISCUSSION
Donald Hall, General Editor

Volumes in the Under Discussion series collect reviews and essays about individual poets. The series is concerned with contemporary American and English poets about whom the consensus has not yet been formed and the final vote has not been taken. Titles in the series include:

Elizabeth Bishop and Her Art
  edited by Lloyd Schwartz and Sybil P. Estess
Richard Wilbur's Creation
  edited and with an Introduction by Wendy Salinger
Reading Adrienne Rich
  edited by Jane Roberta Cooper
On the Poetry of Allen Ginsberg
  edited by Lewis Hyde
Robert Bly: When Sleepers Awake
  edited by Joyce Peseroff
Robert Creeley's Life and Work
  edited by John Wilson
On the Poetry of Galway Kinnell
  edited by Howard Nelson
On Louis Simpson
  edited by Hank Lazer
Anne Sexton
  edited by Steven E. Colburn
James Wright
  edited by Peter Stitt and Frank Graziano
Frank O'Hara
  edited by Jim Elledge

Forthcoming volumes will examine the work of Langston Hughes, Philip Levine, Muriel Rukeyser, H.D., and Denise Levertov, among others.

Please write for further information on available editions and current prices.

Ann Arbor   **The University of Michigan Press**